S0-BVT-688

AMAZING STORIES

GREAT CANADIAN LOVE STORIES

To Grama from Rebecca
August 7/2007

AMAZING STORIES

GREAT CANADIAN LOVE STORIES

Romances, Affairs, and Passionate Tales

ROMANCE/HISTORY

by Cheryl MacDonald

In memory of my parents
Francis William MacDonald
1929–2000
Margaret (Millar) MacDonald
1930–2002

PUBLISHED BY ALTITUDE PUBLISHING CANADA LTD.
1500 Railway Avenue, Canmore, Alberta T1W 1P6
www.altitudepublishing.com
1-800-957-6888

First published 2003

Publisher	Stephen Hutchings
Associate Publisher	Kara Turner
Editor	Dyanne Rivers

We acknowledge the financial support of the Government of Canada through the Book Publishing Industry Development Program (BPIDP) for our publishing activities.

Altitude GreenTree Program
Altitude Publishing will plant twice as many trees as were used in the manufacturing of this product.

National Library of Canada Cataloguing in Publication Data

MacDonald, Cheryl, 1952-
Great Canadian love stories / Cheryl MacDonald

(Amazing stories)
Includes bibliographical references.
ISBN 1-55153-973-X

1. Canada--Biography. I. Title. II. Series: Amazing stories (Canmore, Alta.)

FC25.M333 2003 971'.009'9 C2003-905914-6

Printed and bound in Canada by Friesens
2 4 6 8 9 7 5 3

Cover: The Royal Canadian Mounted Police have always been associated with romance and adventure.

Contents

Prologue

George Washington Johnson wandered through the countryside, soaking in the warmth of the sun. Glad of the respite from his duties, the young schoolteacher was keenly aware of the singing of birds and the lush green meadows dotted with wildflowers. With a poet's sensitivity, he absorbed the details of his surroundings as he contemplated the condition of his own life. He was content, pleased with his position as a country schoolmaster and happy as only a young man in love can be. If there was any cause for dissatisfaction, it was his own ambition. With a little additional experience, he could seek a better job, perhaps in nearby Hamilton, or even in Toronto.

Approaching Twenty Mile Creek, George stopped to rest. Yes, he thought, a better position and marriage to Maggie would make his life perfect. As he watched the water of the creek turn the wheel of a nearby saw-mill, he contemplated his rosy future. Then he frowned. There was one obstacle to a happy future, Maggie's health. If Maggie did not regain her health …

Resolutely, George pushed the gloomy thoughts from his mind. For a time, he watched the hypnotic motion of the wheel, lulled by the distant splash of the water. After a while, some lines of verse came to his mind. Quickly, so as not to lose the inspiration, he pulled a notebook and a pencil from his pocket and began to write about a love that would last a lifetime.

I wander'd to-day to the hill, Maggie …

Chapter 1 Convenient Arrangements

In the past, marriage was often seen as a business or legal arrangement, a means by which one partner might acquire money or property or maintain a family dynasty. Sometimes, arranged marriages led to heartbreak, but in other cases, both partners found some satisfaction and mutual benefit. And now and then, a convenient arrangement blossomed into something more.

One financially motivated marriage had far-reaching implications for the development of Canada. On December 30, 1610, at a church in Paris, France, flickering candlelight revealed the soft lace collars and plumed hats of several prosperous merchants. The men had gathered to watch Hélène Boullé and Samuel de Champlain exchange wedding vows.

Like most 17th-century marriages, this was a business arrangement. The men congratulated Champlain on his shrewdness. His bride brought a dowry of 6,000 livres, enough to assure the survival of the colony at Quebec for the next little while. As investors in the colony that Champlain had founded, the merchants had nearly as much to celebrate as the bridegroom.

Meanwhile, the wedding was the subject of considerable gossip. The sudden marriage of the 40-year-old bachelor was surprising enough. What really raised eyebrows was the knowledge that Hélène, daughter of royal secretary Nicolas Boullé, was barely 12 years old.

A few months earlier, the assassination of King Henri IV had set in a motion a series of events that would change Hélène's life. Henri had supported colonization in New France, and his death had set back the colonial cause. Champlain had left Quebec and returned to Paris in hopes of raising much-needed funds.

Whether or not Champlain deliberately set out to marry for money, his search for funds led directly to Boullé, who had financed the explorer's 1603 expedition. The Canadian adventure was appealing, but the investment was risky. What Boullé needed was a way to protect it.

It happened that Boullé had a daughter of almost marriageable age. A daughter was a great expense — there was the matter of a suitable dowry, for one thing. If Champlain married Hélène, however, Boullé could pay a sizable dowry, which would not only provide needed financing for the colony but also support his daughter. Boullé would no longer be financially responsible for Hélène, and there was always the possibility that the Canadian adventure would make both men very rich.

No one bothered to ask Hélène's opinion. Like all young women of the time, she was expected to obey. Marriage soon after she reached adolescence was the normal course of events. The only respectable alternative was to enter a convent, but because Hélène was a Huguenot, a French Protestant, this option was not open to her.

Given the right circumstances, Hélène might have found the prospect of marriage acceptable. Samuel was physically fit, and he had seen people and places that were just emerging from the mists of legend. And because he frequently dealt with court officials, he displayed a degree of polish and sophistication. But he spent most of his time in the company of men and was often uncomfortable around women.

Still, Hélène might have been intrigued at first, especially when Samuel described the New World to her. Less than three months after the wedding, however, Samuel returned to Quebec. Hélène, left in the care to the care of her parents, soon realized how little her life had changed. On the one hand, marriage had catapulted her into adulthood; on the other, Samuel's absence had pushed her back into childhood, under her parents' strict control. It was a situation calculated to breed discontent.

In Quebec, Champlain explored the St. Lawrence River, discovering a pleasant wooded island near present-day Montreal. He named it Ile-Ste- Hélène, after his bride's patron saint. As autumn settled in, he sailed for France carrying gifts for Hélène, including a pair of beaded moccasins and a sweetgrass basket decorated with porcupine quills.

Samuel lingered in Paris for a year, finally sailing for Quebec in March 1613. During his winter in France, he had basked in the prestige brought about by the publication of a book about his explorations. Unfortunately, his triumph was short-lived, overshadowed by a personal crisis. In the fall of 1613, Hélène deserted him.

She was nearly 16, an adult by the standards of the time. With youth, good breeding and fine clothes on her side, Hélène was at her most attractive. Yet she was tied to a man three times her age, a man whose frequent absences forced her to remain under parental supervision. The situation was intolerable. After making her unhappiness clear, Hélène ran away.

For some time, no one could locate her. There were no shelters for women, except convents, and a wife needed her husband's permission to enter one. Hélène could not stay with a woman friend, because women had few legal rights. Responsibility for Hélène's presence would fall on the woman's father or husband — and no man would undermine his position in society by sheltering a rebellious wife. Besides, both Samuel and her father had powerful friends. Few would risk their anger by protecting Hélène.

Did she have a lover to whom she fled? An amorous gentleman with keen powers of observation could not help but notice that Hélène was both attractive and unhappy. A smile, sympathetic words, and whispered endearments while walking or watching a pageant, impassioned love notes delivered by a willing maidservant, kisses stolen behind a pillar or some artfully arranged shrubbery — all would have been possible. The need for secrecy would have added excitement to the courtship, excitement of a kind Hélène had never experienced.

Sadly, her dreams of romance would have vanished quickly as the precariousness of her situation became evident. A wife and daughter, no matter how recalcitrant, must be provided for, fed, clothed, and sheltered. A mistress could be cast aside. Ultimately, Hélène had no choice but to return home.

On January 10, 1614, Boullé and his wife formally disinherited their daughter, testifying that she had shamed them with her rebelliousness, her refusal to live peacefully with her husband, and her flight from their home. Adultery was not mentioned in the legal documents. If Hélène had been unfaithful, it was not in the best interests of Champlain or his in-laws to make this known. Still, there were oblique references to an "unmentionable" crime and Hélène's "scandalous" and "atrocious" remarks. The unhappy young woman had bitterly disappointed both her husband and her parents.

Despite her parents' drastic legal action, Hélène remained in their household while Champlain sailed in and out of her life. Then, in 1620, after nearly a decade of marriage, Hélène faced a new ordeal when she travelled to Quebec with her husband.

This was no pleasure cruise. Aside from daily Mass and whatever songs or music the crew and passengers could provide, there was little diversion on board the ship. Provisions consisted mainly of salted fish and meat, hard biscuits, water, and wine. By the end of the voyage, the biscuits were wormy, the water stagnant. The ship pitched terribly, and Hélène was often seasick. By the time they reached Tadoussac, in the Gulf of St. Lawrence, she was wretched.

The next day, however, there was cause for celebration. A small boat approached the ship, and among its passengers was Eustache, Hélène's brother, who had accompanied Samuel to Quebec two years earlier.

"Sieur Boullé, my brother-in-law ... was greatly surprised to see his sister and to think that she could have made up her mind to cross so stormy a sea," Champlain recorded in his journal. "He was greatly pleased, and she and I were still more so."

Even her brother's presence, however, could not make up for the conditions Hélène found in Quebec. Sixty French and assorted Aboriginal people gathered to welcome Samuel and his young wife. The next day, the two inspected the habitation, the fortress-like dwelling that was Samuel's Quebec headquarters. It was a shambles, as Samuel reported in his journal.

> *I found this settlement of ours in fact in such an abandoned and ruinous condition that I felt grieved. The rain was coming in everywhere; the wind blew through all the crevices of the planks, which had shrunk as time went on, the store-*

> *house upon the point of tumbling down; ... the whole looked like some poor abandoned tenement in the fields.*

If Samuel was grieved, his wife was devastated. This was nothing like the sturdy shelter he had described. Hélène burst into tears.

As the colony absorbed her husband's attention, Hélène grew restless. After the bustle of Paris, Quebec was unbearably dull. She had no female companions — her servants did not count, and the other women in the colony were far beneath her socially. She had no children to occupy her time, and housework was done by servants. Her only amusements were walking, a little gardening, attending Mass, and befriending the Aboriginal people.

The winter of 1623–24 was especially difficult. The colony was short of supplies, and by June, had almost run out of flour and cider. By the time supply ships arrived in July, Hélène had had her fill of New France.

In October, she and Samuel returned to Paris, where he found a home in *le Temple,* an ancient quarter of the city. Though he may have intended to settle down, he soon found himself longing for the pristine beauty of New France.

Hélène did nothing to change his mind. Although the fire that had flared into rebellion in her youth was subsiding, she was still unhappy in the marriage. In the first years after the wedding, she had clung stubbornly to her Huguenot beliefs, but later converted to Catholicism. Now she asked Samuel's permission to enter a convent, the only form of marital separation available to Catholics of the era. Her husband refused her request. His return to Quebec in 1626 was the final act in a relationship that had been falling apart for years.

A twist of fate brought Samuel and Hélène together one last time. In July 1629, Quebec was captured by the English. Samuel was taken to England as a prisoner, only to learn that the war that had provoked the attack had ended in April, making the conquest illegal. He hurried to Paris to ensure that Canada was returned to France and placed under his control.

During his visit, Hélène again asked to enter a convent and was again refused. Samuel did, however, provide for her financial security before leaving for Quebec in March 1633.

Samuel died on Christmas Day 1635 and was buried in the colony to which he had devoted much of his life. Though Hélène was now a wealthy widow, she still dreamed of entering a convent, and in 1645, this dream was fulfilled. She joined the Ursulines as Sister Hélène de Saint-Augustin. Three years later, she founded a new convent at Meaux, northeast of Paris.

For the next six years, Sister Hélène led a life of quiet contemplation, far from the Paris she had known as a girl — and farther still from the colony at Quebec where other Ursulines were teaching French and Aboriginal children. Did Hélène ever pray for the colony or for the soul of its founder, the husband she had never loved? Did she ask forgiveness for the sins she had committed in her lifetime? Whatever thoughts and whatever secrets she possessed about Samuel de Champlain and the bitter disappointment of their marriage died with her on December 20, 1654.

In the century after Hélène's death, Quebec grew into a place of tidy farms and flourishing businesses. Though most inhabitants made their living from the land or the fur trade, there was also a strong military presence in the colony.

On January 26, 1751, Jean Corolère went to have a drink at a local tavern. The 20-year-old was a drummer in a grenadier and gunnery company in Quebec City. Many of his comrades-in-arms were present at Laforme's tavern, and in the course of the evening, a disagreement erupted. Some of the other soldiers insulted him.

Particularly irked by the comments of a fellow named Coffre, Jean promptly challenged him to a duel.

That very night, the two young men faced each other, swords drawn, faces serious. Someone gave the word and metal clanged against metal.

Almost instantly, Jean cut the fingers of Coffre's right hand, drawing blood. Satisfied that they had acquitted themselves honourably, the two ended the duel and returned to the tavern. As far as they were concerned, the matter was over. But duelling was illegal in New France, and when word reached the authorities, warrants were issued for the arrest of the two men. Coffre vanished without a trace, but Jean was tossed into prison.

For five agonizing months, he waited in a cold, damp cell, convinced he would freeze to death or starve on the standard prison fare of bread and water. Finally, on June 2, 1751, he appeared before a court and was sentenced to a year in prison.

The prospect of spending 12 more months in jail plunged Jean into despair. Then, miraculously, salvation presented itself in the shapely form of another prisoner.

Occupying the cell next to Jean's was Françoise Laurent, the daughter of a drum major. In October 1750, several weeks before Jean's ill-advised duel, she had been convicted of stealing clothes from her employers, the Pommereaus. The penalty for theft was death. But before the sentence could be carried out, the colony's executioner died. Because no successor had been named, Françoise was condemned to an indefinite term in prison, never certain whether her next breath of fresh air would be on her way to the gallows.

But Françoise was a careful planner who was also willing to take a risk. She had gambled on stealing clothes from Mme Pommereau without getting caught, and she had lost. This time, she was determined to win.

With the help of the jailer, the condemned woman cultivated a friendship with Jean. They were close to the same age, and Françoise's charms were enhanced by Jean's realization that few other women would look favourably upon a convict. To Jean, it seemed that she was the only woman in the colony who truly understood his plight. And he certainly empathized with hers. In desperation, the young prisoners came to rely more and more on each other, and soon they were lovers.

As the cool Canadian spring yielded to the searing heat of summer, Jean and Françoise shared stolen kisses and bittersweet embraces, fully aware they would be parted forever when Jean's sentence ended. Then one day, Françoise suggested a bold plan.

In New France, a tradition allowed a prisoner who accepted the executioner's duties to go free. Françoise urged Jean to apply for the job and save himself before he wasted away in prison. Besides, she pointed out, once he was free, he might be able to help her.

Jean was torn. Executioners were a necessary evil, but hardly the kind of people others wanted to be friendly with. But eventually he agreed. On August 17, 1751, he petitioned the colonial authorities to accept him as executioner. His request was quickly granted. Jean was released and went to live in the house that was provided as part of his salary.

Meanwhile, Françoise lingered in jail, anxiously awaiting news. Although Jean had pledged his undying love while in prison, he might lose interest. Would another young woman, one unblemished by imprisonment and a death sentence, catch his eye? The hours after Jean's release seemed infinitely longer than the months Françoise had already spent in prison.

Fortunately, her worries were unfounded. Jean had not forgotten his promise. The day after his release, he petitioned the courts. Precious as they were, he declared, freedom and financial security were not enough. Even an executioner needed a wife, a mother for the children so desperately needed to populate the colony. He would have no other wife than Françoise Laurent — but she was condemned to death, and how could he execute the woman he loved? He begged for her release, asking the authorities to allow him to marry and set up a respectable home.

The answer came swiftly. Françoise's death sentence was revoked, and she was set free. On August 19, 1751, Jean and Françoise were married in the intendant's palace, forging the final link in a chain begun in the chilly darkness of a prison cell.

Eight years after Jean and Françoise wed, French forces were defeated on the Plains of Abraham. Canada became an English colony, protected by British soldiers and sailors. Among them were members of the royal family, including Edward Augustus, fourth son of King George III.

Born on November 1, 1767, Edward had been sent to Europe for military training at the age of 15. The teenager grew into a tall, blue-eyed, blond young man, who was a hard-working, conscientious soldier. His looks and credentials as a prince meant that there was always an attractive woman or two in his life.

One woman in particular caught Edward's eye. She was Adelaide Dubus, a French actress. They had an affair, and in 1789, Adelaide became pregnant with Edward's child. Tragically, she died after giving birth to a daughter. When news of the scandal reached England, the king punished Edward by sending him to the English military base at Gibraltar. He arrived in 1790.

Aside from taverns, there was little in the way of

entertainment on the rock guarding the western entrance to the Mediterranean, and Edward was never a heavy drinker. During the first weeks after his arrival, he busied himself learning his duties, making new acquaintances, and setting up his modest household. By June, he was writing to his brother George, the Prince of Wales, that he was lonely. What he needed, he confessed, was a female companion.

Edward sent for Victoire Dubus, sister of his deceased mistress, and his infant daughter. Apparently, he hoped that Victoire would take Adelaide's place and that they could lead a pleasant family life with the baby. But the child died en route from Marseilles, and Victoire was unwilling to share the prince's bed.

Undaunted, Edward sent his valet, Fontiny, to shop for a suitable companion. He even provided a list of requirements. The young woman must be attractive and well-mannered. A love of music was essential, for music was one of Edward's great joys.

Fontiny found a willing candidate in Thérèse-Bernardine Mongenet, also known as Julie. He hired her as a singer to give a veneer of respectability to the proposed arrangement. He also found lodgings for Julie in town. Edward would have none of it. He wanted his companion to share his house, and after scolding his valet, sent a warm message to the young woman, expressing his eagerness to meet her and warning her to expect the modest accommodations of a soldier rather than the luxurious home of a prince. (Edward was, in fact, constantly in debt.)

Fortunately, Julie was no stranger to the military lifestyle. She had been born into a bourgeois family in Besançon, a French military town. Some time in her late teens or early 20s, she had become the mistress of the Baron de Fortisson and had then moved on to the Marquis de Permangle. Julie stayed with Permangle until the upheaval of the French Revolution reduced him to making salads for a living. Unwilling to give up the lifestyle she had become accustomed to, Julie left. She was still unattached when Fontiny presented Edward's offer.

Julie's arrival in Gibraltar toward the end of 1790 raised eyebrows. Some of the senior officers knew her by reputation. In 20th-century terms, she was considered a gold-digger, a woman of dubious morals. She was also was seven years older than the prince. There were suggestions that she be bribed to leave.

Whether a bribe was ever offered is unrecorded. What is known is that Julie made the prince happy. By early 1791, he was writing to his brother William, Duke of Clarence, that his new companion was sweet-tempered, clever, and attractive.

In 1791, the prince's regiment was ordered to Canada. The troop ships set sail with the prince, his servants, and Julie — under the name Mme de Saint-Laurent — on board. In Quebec, Edward received a warm welcome. Public dinners and receptions were held in his honour. Julie, of course, was not invited. As a royal mistress, her position was ambiguous, and Edward would not force her presence on anyone who might be made uncomfortable by their relationship. But the Prince also enjoyed a private social life. Julie hosted dinners at Edward's home, and together, they attended social functions at which Edward was not appearing in an official capacity.

Edward and Julie's behaviour was guided by precedents set by Edward's older brothers. William had established a household with an actress, Dorothea Jordan, who bore him 10 children. And George had married his mistress, Maria Fitzherbert, a charming and aristocratic woman who was, unfortunately, Roman Catholic. Though Maria took solace in the wedding ceremony, the marriage was not legally binding. No member of the royal family could marry without the permission of the sovereign, and this had not been granted. Nevertheless, London society found acceptable ways of dealing with these two liaisons without offending either the princes or public morals — and the people of Quebec took their cue from London.

Edward and Julie had much in common. They shared a love of music and literature and often spent enjoyable evenings alone together, reading or singing duets. At the same time, Julie was completely able to amuse herself when duty called Edward away. In addition to writing letters, she kept a journal, visited friends, and sewed most of her own clothes.

For his part, Edward treated his mistress with all the respect and consideration due a wife. In fact, Julie was so much like a wife, that, like other husbands of his time and class, Edward was unfaithful. His brief affair with Eliza Green produced a child but did not result in a serious rift with Julie.

Like any soldier's wife, Julie also endured periods of separation. When Edward was posted to the West Indies in 1793, she went to England. They were reunited a short time later in Halifax, where Julie impressed Nova Scotia governor John Wentworth and his wife. Wentworth wrote about her: "She is an elegant, well bred, pleasing, sensible woman — far beyond most ... She seemed faithfully attached to [Edward]."

Julie and Edward stayed in Halifax for several months. They lived at first with the Wentworths, then rented the governor's country house on Bedford Basin, about 10 kilometres outside town. Wentworth called the place Friar Laurence's Cell, a reference to the meeting place of Romeo and Juliet, and there, Edward and Julie spent some of their happiest hours. Always eager to beautify his surroundings, Edward redecorated and landscaped. According to local legend, he planned the paths through the woods behind the house so they spelled out "Julie."

Although they were content, Edward had been longing to return to England. But military duties, as well as his father's reluctance to summon him home, had kept him abroad. In August 1798, his horse threw him, then rolled on top of him. Though the injury healed slowly and left him with a pronounced limp, his convalescence gave him an opportunity to sail for England.

He and Julie arrived on November 14. Careful to avoid scandal, especially with his father so near, Edward arranged separate accommodations for Julie. The couple rarely appeared together in public, but when King George III gave Edward the title Duke of Kent — and the generous income that went with the honour — one of the new duke's first actions was to ensure that Julie was financially secure.

The next year, the couple was back in Nova Scotia, although Edward was now bothered by rheumatism and wanted to go home. Eventually, he was able to obtain a leave of absence and return to England. There, he bought Julie an estate at Ealing. Nestled on about 12 hectares, Castle Hill Lodge had belonged to Maria Fitzherbert and, like the house on Bedford Basin, provided a happy home for the couple.

After two pleasant years in England, Edward was appointed governor of Gibraltar and commander of the military post there. Though the return to the place of their first meeting must have aroused warm memories for the couple, a mutiny among the troops marred Edward's posting to the rock, and he was recalled to England.

Despite the incident, Edward and Julie found a measure of contentment at Castle Hill Lodge. Most mornings, they breakfasted alone, quietly reading the newspapers. Edward became increasingly involved in charitable work, and Julie, as always, kept busy running the household, writing to friends and relatives, reading, and sewing her own clothes. Their life was serene and pleasant. But clouds were gathering on their horizon.

Royal advisers and the newspapers were making increasingly loud noises about the question of succession. Of all George III's children, only the Prince of Wales had produced a legitimate heir, Princess Charlotte. And so began a flurry of marriages in an effort to secure the throne of England.

For a long time, Edward had probably felt little

pressure to marry suitably. After all, he had three older brothers. Now, the need to make a suitable union became more pressing for two reasons. First, it would help ensure the succession. Second, as a married prince, Edward could expect his income to increase, an important consideration for a man who was heavily in debt.

Edward may have made some half-hearted marriage inquiries, though he seems to have dropped them when his niece Charlotte married. At any rate, he and Julie decided to spend time abroad, and in the fall of 1816, they settled into a hotel in Brussels.

By early 1817, rumours that Edward would marry were becoming stronger. Early in February, Julie read a newspaper report on the subject. She was hurt by the rumours, and her reaction pained Edward deeply.

Matters came to a head when Princess Charlotte died in childbirth in November 1817. Within a short time, rumours of Edward's impending engagement reached the press.

In fact, the negotiations for his betrothal had been under way for some time. His prospective bride, Victoire Maria Louisa, Princess of Leiningen, was a widow with two children. Despite these developments, however, Edward refused to discuss the situation with Julie. Instead, he asked a trusted friend to write a letter requesting his return to England on official business.

When Edward left Brussels in March 1818, Julie travelled to Paris to visit her sister. She must have been suspicious, worried that her happy life with the prince was coming to an end, but she struggled to maintain her dignity. This struggle would have become nearly impossible when Edward married in July.

At first, Julie could not bear any mention of the marriage, though she gradually became reconciled to the idea. She and Edward corresponded, and he urged old friends to call on her and to be especially kind. Duty and pressing financial problems may have forced him to marry, but Edward would not tolerate mistreatment of his "beloved companion of eight and twenty years."

On May 24, 1819, Edward's wife gave birth to a daughter, Alexandrina Victoria. Much later, as Queen Victoria, this child would lend her name to an age that exalted respectability and family values.

Having done his duty by providing an heir to the throne, Edward might well have considered returning to Julie, or at least visiting her. But fate intervened. Edward caught cold, and despite his generally good health, succumbed to the infection. He died on January 24, 1820, at the age of 52.

For Julie, his death was a terrible blow. Yet she drew comfort from the knowledge that he had spoken of her to his new wife in the kindest terms. In a remarkable gesture of compassion, the duchess wrote a letter of condolence to her husband's former mistress. In addition, she made certain that Julie received the money Edward had set aside for her.

Julie continued to live quietly in Paris, visited by friends who had known both her and Edward in the old, happy days. After a brief illness, she died on August 8, 1830, and was buried beside her sister in Père Lachaise cemetery.

Chapter 2
Tragic Romances

Romeo and Juliet were not the world's first — or last — star-crossed lovers. Despite hopeful beginnings and valiant efforts, some romances are doomed to failure. One of these was recorded in Queen Marguerite of Angoulème's *L'Heptameron des nouvelles.* It told the story of a young Frenchwoman, Marguerite de La Rocque.

In 1542, Marguerite was one of a party of settlers who were attempting to colonize the New World as part of an expedition led by her uncle, Jean-François de La Rocque de Roberval.

The aristocratic Roberval was well known at the court of Francis I, the French king. A former soldier,

Roberval was one of many devil-may-care young men who squandered a fortune in the pursuit of pleasure. By the time he was 40, he was in serious financial trouble and faced the prospect of selling his ancestral lands to pay his creditors. Across the Atlantic lay an unknown land of fabled wealth — and perhaps the passage to the Indies that so many had sought. Certain that he would be able to rebuild his fortune, the adventurer persuaded King Francis to finance an expedition to the New World.

In January 1540, Roberval received his commission and enough money to outfit a company to explore and settle the New World. Although he had once made his living as a pirate, his second in command was vastly more qualified to lead the expedition. Jacques Cartier had already made two trips to the New World, the last in 1536. He was probably the most accomplished navigator in France and was certainly the best informed about the lands across the Atlantic Ocean.

What Cartier thought about Roberval's leadership is unknown. What is known is that the two had trouble recruiting volunteers for the expedition. Although a few gentleman adventurers enlisted, Roberval and Cartier were reduced to drafting condemned prisoners to make up the balance.

Cartier set sail in the spring of 1541, while Roberval lingered in France to wind up some business. By April 16 of the following year, he was ready to set out with three ships and a group of 200 would-be settlers. Among the handful of women on board was his niece Marguerite.

An heiress in her own right, the young woman was accompanied by a female servant, Damienne. Although Marguerite had joined the company voluntarily, her reason for doing so is unclear. Perhaps, like her uncle, she was attracted by the promise of riches beyond imagining. Perhaps she was hungry for adventure. Or, given the events that soon transpired, perhaps she chose to be close to the man she loved.

The passengers on Roberval's ships rested in the area of St. John's, Newfoundland, for several days, recuperating from the effects of the tempestuous eight-week crossing. To their surprise, they soon spotted Cartier's ships, which were on their way back to France. Cartier had taken on a cargo of what he thought was gold and diamonds, but which eventually proved to be fool's gold and quartz. He wanted to take the treasure home, and besides, he warned, trouble was brewing with the Aboriginal people he had met.

Roberval ordered Cartier to turn around and sail back up the St. Lawrence. Cartier ignored him and headed for France, leaving the angry nobleman to start a colony on his own. This would not be easy. Uniting an ill-assorted collection of adventurers and criminals was difficult in itself. Now Cartier had undermined his authority. Roberval also found himself arbitrating disputes between the Portuguese and Basque fishermen in the harbour. And then, to make matters worse, he discovered his niece was conducting a passionate love affair.

On its own, Marguerite's liaison was hardly cause for disapproval. At the French court, illicit love affairs were a normal part of life for aristocratic women. More than the affair itself, Roberval probably disapproved of Marguerite's choice, whose name has been lost to history. As her guardian, at least for the duration of the expedition, Roberval would have kept his niece's marriage prospects firmly in mind. Was the lover one of the gentlemen adventurers, perhaps an impoverished nobleman who could offer little in the way of financial security? Or was he one of the reprieved criminals, a thief or worse, who could offer the young woman even less? If he had learned of the liaison, Roberval may have warned the lovers to end the relationship. Perhaps their disobedience gave him an excuse to impose a harsh punishment.

Because so many of his colonists were convicted felons, Roberval found it necessary to rule his company with an iron hand. One man was hanged for theft, another clapped into irons, and several others were whipped. These punishments were typical of the times.

But what could Roberval do about his disobedient and deceitful niece?

Sometime in July, Roberval's company set sail for the Strait of Belle Isle. By this time, Marguerite was pregnant. Determined to punish her, Roberval stopped the ships at an island, probably Fogo, off the northeast corner of Newfoundland. He put the couple — and the loyal Damienne — ashore with enough supplies to enable them to survive. Then he sailed with the rest of the company to their winter encampment.

Marooned on the island, Marguerite and her lover turned their attention to survival. With a little effort, they could manage. Fogo had fresh water and woods stocked with game and fruit. Besides, there was always the hope that a fishing vessel would rescue them.

Marguerite was ill-prepared for life in the wilderness, but she was strong and intelligent enough to work with the materials at hand. As autumn drew near, the trio built a log hut. Using the muskets Roberval had given them, they shot animals, tanning the hides for clothing and eating the meat. Although none of the three had experienced a Canadian winter, they had probably heard stories from members of Cartier's company, and they prepared for the worst they could imagine.

Whatever they had imagined, it probably fell short of the reality. Like most early colonists, they no doubt underestimated the harshness of Canada's winter, the driving winds, bitter temperatures, and freezing storms. Eventually, their small supply of food ran out, and they were forced to eat whatever they could find. Sometimes, they were fortunate. The ice floes brought seals close to shore and, on one occasion, a polar bear. But a steady diet of fresh meat is not healthy. Long before spring arrived, Marguerite's lover had fallen ill, probably of scurvy.

He died around the beginning of March. Shortly afterwards, she gave birth to their child, and the arrival of spring encouraged her to hope that a ship would appear. But spring turned slowly to summer without any sign of rescue. Then the second fall arrived, and both the infant and Damienne died, leaving Marguerite alone.

Determination and her hunting skill kept Marguerite alive through another winter. A second summer passed, and, finally, in September, a fishing vessel reached the island and carried her back to France.

Meanwhile, Roberval's colony had failed, and with it, his dream of making a quick fortune. Returning to France, he spent several years fighting lawsuits before being murdered by a mob in 1560.

Nothing is known of Marguerite's later life. But others learned of her adventure, which was immortalized in a book of love stories prepared by Queen Marguerite, sister of King Francis. Inspired by Boccacio's

Decameron, the *Heptameron* was read avidly in France.

Marguerite de La Rocque's love affair ended in tragedy because of the direct interference of someone close to her. Other lovers, among them two young people from Acadia, have found themselves torn apart by the impersonal forces of history.

In the early 1700s, the fate of Acadia hung in the balance. As Britain and France fought for control of North America, the French-speaking Acadians who farmed and fished in what is now Nova Scotia and New Brunswick maintained their traditional way of life. Then, in the summer and fall of 1755, British conquerors forced them out of their homes.

Five times between 1680 and 1730, the Acadians had been asked to take an oath of loyalty to the British crown. Five times they had refused — unless they were allowed to add a clause exempting them from military service. Finally, in 1730, Governor Richard Phillips compromised by allowing them to swear an oath that made no mention of taking up arms for the British. Twenty-five years later, Governor Charles Lawrence found this compromise unacceptable and demanded that the Acadians swear an unaltered oath. Again they refused, this time with disastrous consequences.

The British assembled a fleet of ships, ready to

transport anyone who refused to take the oath. In some places where men had gathered to protest, soldiers were ordered to deport them before their wives and families arrived Moved by compassion, a few British soldiers did what little they could to lessen the trauma of upheaval. Most simply followed orders, however, pursuing Acadians who hid in the woods and putting farms and fields to the torch so that none could return to their homes.

By the end of 1755, nearly 7,000 people had been torn from their homes, separated from family and friends, and exiled to British colonies in New England, Maryland, Virginia, Georgia, and the Carolinas. Forbidden to return to Acadia, some settled permanently in their new locations, notably in Louisiana where they became known as Cajuns. Others overcame incredible obstacles to find loved ones, and a handful made their way back home.

As the years passed, stories of the hardships endured by the exiles became a part of North American folklore. Nearly a hundred years after the expulsion, American poet Henry Wadsworth Longfellow heard the story and used it as the basis for his epic poem, "Evangeline."

The poem tells the story of childhood sweethearts, Evangeline Bellefontaine and Gabrielle Lajeunesse.

After the expulsion, Evangeline spends years searching for her lost love and, having reconciled herself to losing him, becomes a nurse. During an epidemic, she finds Gabriel among the victims. Reunited, the lovers have time for one last kiss before Gabriel dies.

The poem captured the public imagination, ensuring that the tragedy of the Acadians would never be forgotten. It also sparked a search for the "real" Evangeline.

Though nearly every story turns out to be partly fictional, the legends persist, perhaps because they contain a large grain of truth. Somehow, in the chaos and confusion of deportation, at least one pair of lovers must have become separated. And perhaps, many years later, they were reunited. Without solid documentary evidence, their names remain unknown. But a traditional account from Louisiana probably comes as close as any to capturing the spirit of the legend.

Her name was Emmeline Labische, and at the time of the expulsion, she was engaged to Louis Arsenaux, her childhood sweetheart. Just 16 years old, Emmeline was a sweet-tempered, loving young woman, who was torn from all she knew and cherished just hours before her wedding. Eventually, she found herself in Maryland. Meanwhile, Louis was in Louisiana, nearly 2,000 kilometres away.

Like Longfellow's Evangeline, Emmeline searched

ceaselessly for her lover. She seized on this clue, that rumour, always disappointed but never giving up hope. Several years later, she reached Louisiana. And suddenly, there he was, older and a little careworn, but still her Louis.

Emmeline rushed toward him, arms outstretched. Louis turned away, but not before she had seen the look of recognition on his face — and something else. Bewildered, she questioned him. Reluctantly, Louis confessed that he had married another.

Emmeline was overwhelmed. She had survived the loss of her home, the loss of her family, and the wrenching separation from the only man she had ever loved, the only man she *could* ever love. And now this.

Emmeline's grip on reality began to slip away. The bitter disappointment drove her mad, and she died soon afterwards.

Just as Emmeline's tragic story inspired a well-known poem, another romance led to the creation of a popular song. But in this case, the words were written by one of the participants. During his courtship of Maggie Clarke, schoolteacher George Washington Johnson penned the verses that defied death and immortalized their love.

Born in 1839 in Binbrook, Ontario, a farming community southeast of Hamilton, George grew up on the family farm. As a youngster, he showed a talent for writing, especially for writing poetry, a gift he later attributed to his mixed Irish and Mohawk heritage.

In 1854 or 1855, George began teaching school in nearby Welland County and eventually went on to study at the University of Toronto. Returning to teaching, he found a post in Glanford, not far from his hometown.

As a prominent member of the community, the young schoolmaster was the focus of considerable attention. Young and well educated, he was a handsome man with dark eyes and dark curly hair. A Glanford girl could do worse than to marry young Mr. Johnson, and many of the local belles may have vied to catch his eye.

Soon, however, everyone knew that George had found a sweetheart. Maggie Clarke was one of his pupils, a slender young woman with beautiful blonde ringlets. Born on July 14, 1841, Maggie was the eldest daughter of Joseph Clarke, a prosperous farmer and sawmill owner.

Lively and popular, Maggie had many friends, who often gathered at the Clarke farm to chat or sing, or otherwise amuse themselves. But Maggie also had a serious side, for she planned to become a teacher.

Whether it was Maggie's youthful good looks, her scholarly ability, or her love of music that first attracted George, the two soon became a couple. In addition to singing together, they also took long walks through the countryside, discussing their hopes and dreams for the future.

Maggie's health was fragile, however, and her illness cast a shadow on their dreams more than once. Still, with the buoyant optimism of youth, they tried to ignore the threat to their happiness. Sometimes, though, this was impossible, particularly when Maggie's ailment sapped her strength, confining her to bed. Then George walked the familiar meadows alone. It was probably on one of these occasions that he wrote a poem reflecting his fervent wish that he and Maggie would grow old together. The poem's poignant first verse describes his dream.

I wander'd to-day to the hill, Maggie
To watch the scene below,
The creek and the creaking old mill, Maggie
As we used to long ago.
The green grove is gone from the hill, Maggie,
Where first the daisies sprung,
The creaking old mill is still, Maggie
Since you and I were young.

George must have shown the verses to Maggie, along with other love poems he had written. Doubtlessly touched, she may have kept copies with her during their separation, while she studied at Wesleyan College in Hamilton. Certainly, she must have been pleased to learn that George planned to collect several of the poems in a book, *Maple Leaves,* which was published in 1864.

How proud she was of George! And how much prouder still when they were married on October 21 of the same year at the Methodist Church in Glanford Township.

At about this time, George decided to change careers and accepted a position as a journalist with the *Buffalo Courier.* Not long afterwards, he moved to the *Cleveland Plain Dealer.* In Ohio's largest city, there were plenty of opportunities for a young, energetic, and ambitious man.

With an exciting new job and a loving wife, George's happiness seemed assured. Tragically, his life with Maggie was all too brief. Her illness flared up again, and this time there was nothing doctors could do. On May 12, 1865, she died of tuberculosis, just two months short of her 24th birthday and a scant six months since her marriage.

Heartbroken, George took Maggie's body back to Glanford and her grieving family. Perhaps because Canada held the memory of happier days or perhaps because there, near her grave in the Clarke family plot at the White Church Cemetery, he could feel closer to

Maggie, George decided against returning to the United States. For a time, he worked at the *Hamilton Spectator*, but he eventually resumed his teaching career in Binbrook. And he continued to write poetry. At times, it seemed as if he could almost sense Maggie's presence, for on the flyleaf of *Maple Leaves*, he inscribed these lines from a poem by Henry Wadsworth Longfellow:

With a slow and noiseless footstep
Comes this messenger divine,
Takes the vacant place beside me,
Lays her gentle hand in mine.

While George was haunted by memories of his lost love, his book was enjoying some popularity. A copy came to the attention of American composer James Austin Butterfield, who was so touched by "When You and I Were Young, Maggie" that he set the words to music in 1865.

Though the song became a great success, George received no money from it. He spent the rest of his life as a teacher, rising to be principal of Central School in Hamilton. In 1891, he joined the staff of Toronto's Upper Canada College, where he headed the commercial department. And though he remarried twice, he never forgot Maggie — or the love immortalized in a song that is still sung in the 21st century.

Chapter 3
Defying Convention

For centuries, societies frowned on romances between lovers of different classes, different races, and different religions. Yet lovers have always been willing to bridge the gap. Among them was Sheila O'Connor, an Irish princess who married a pirate.

Early in 1602, Sheila set sail from her home in Ireland's County Connaught. Bound for a French convent, she had no idea that she was setting out on an adventure that would make her famous throughout Newfoundland as Sheila Nagira — Sheila the Fair — the Irish princess.

The reason Sheila was to enter the convent has

been forgotten. Perhaps she felt drawn to a religious life, and the convent where her aunt was abbess seemed an appropriate place to begin her vocation. More likely, Sheila was being sent to safety. In the last years of the reign of Elizabeth I of England, Ireland was the scene of many bloody battles. A French convent may have seemed like a safe refuge for a young woman who could trace her ancestry to the ancient kings of Ireland.

The green hills of Ireland had scarcely faded from the horizon when Sheila's ship was attacked by a Dutch privateer. Because the Irish ship was unarmed, its captain had no choice but to surrender, and the passengers and crew were taken aboard the Dutch vessel. Some were chained on deck or in the stinking hold, although the more privileged, including Sheila, were allowed a certain amount of freedom.

Piracy was common in the 17th century. In many instances, the pirates were actually privateers, agents of the Crown, who were handsomely rewarded for harassing enemy ships. This seems to have been the motivation of the Dutch captain, and it was certainly the motivation of Captain Peter Easton, who attacked the Dutch vessel a few days later.

Easton was an English gentleman. When he met the Dutch privateer in the English Channel, he was leading a small convoy to Newfoundland. As the three

English ships bore down on the Dutch vessel, panic overwhelmed Sheila and the other captives. If the captain chose to fight, they would be helpless before the English cannons. A single ball could rip a hole in the side of the wooden ship and send its luckless passengers to the bottom of the channel. And if the English sailors boarded, who knew what havoc they might wreak with swords and cutlasses before the terrified prisoners could explain their situation?

Fortunately, the Dutch captain was more businessman than buccaneer. He surrendered. The captives were freed, and their captors imprisoned aboard the English ship. Easton had no intention of letting the minor skirmish interfere with his orders, however. He was bound for Newfoundland, where English fishermen and entrepreneurs needed his protection against French and Portuguese rivals.

And so Sheila made an unexpected detour, crossing the Atlantic instead of sailing to France. As the ships navigated the grey ocean waters, Sheila became friendly with Gilbert Pike, one of Easton's young lieutenants. Their friendship quickly blossomed into love.

Within 10 days of meeting, the couple stood together on the swaying deck. Surrounded by salt spray instead of the perfume of flowers, Gilbert and Sheila became man and wife.

Under normal circumstances, Sheila and her husband would have spent only a short time in Newfoundland, a year or two at most, before returning to England. But Queen Elizabeth died in 1603, and her successor, King James I, made peace with Spain. Privateers were no longer considered necessary, and Gilbert and his comrades found themselves unemployed. Sheila and Gilbert moved to Mosquito, now Bristol's Hope, on Conception Bay. There, they settled and made a living from the sea.

Several years later, pirates attacked the settlement. This time, Sheila escaped with her husband and child to an island fortress at Carbonear.

According to Newfoundland tradition, Sheila lived to be more than 100, long enough to see her numerous descendants spread throughout Newfoundland, carrying with them the story of Sheila Nagira and her adventures on the high seas.

As European settlers spread across Canada, the new arrivals frequently came into contact with Aboriginal people. Although they often lived in harmony, there were also many cases of friction and racial prejudice. In 1832, Peter Jones described the prejudice that existed in Upper Canada in a letter to his English fiancée. "They think it is not right for the whites to intermarry with Indians," he warned.

The son of a Welsh-American surveyor and a Mississauga woman, Peter had experience racial prejudice firsthand. Although many white men married Aboriginal women to expand their landholdings, these unions were frowned on. It was considered even more disgraceful for a white woman to marry an Aboriginal man.

For Peter and Elizabeth Field, race was only one of the obstacles standing in the way of their marriage. Elizabeth, often called Eliza, was the daughter of wealthy English soap and candle maker. She was well educated and seemed destined for a life of comfortable gentility. But Eliza was also deeply religious, determined to make her life meaningful in the service of others.

In June 1831, shortly after her 27th birthday, Eliza visited friends in Bristol. There, she met Peter Jones, a young missionary from Upper Canada. He had been sent to Britain on a fund-raising tour.

Peter belonged to the Methodist Episcopalian church, one of several Christian churches dedicated to bringing the Gospel to the Aboriginal peoples of North America. The 29-year-old was a walking advertisement for the success of missionary ventures. As Kahkewaquonaby, Sacred Feathers, he had spent his early years among the Mississauga, following their spiritual traditions. In 1823, he had converted to Methodism and become the first Methodist missionary to the Mississaugas of the Credit River.

Eliza was impressed by the handsome, well-spoken, and humble young man. Despite their religious differences — Eliza was Anglican — she wanted to help with Peter's missionary work. As time passed, she realized that she was in love, and that Peter returned her feelings. On February 2, 1832, she wrote in her diary, "I feel as tho' I could lay open all my heart to the friend I love." Soon afterward, Peter proposed.

Eliza gladly accepted, but as a dutiful daughter, she would not marry without the blessing of her father and stepmother. They were not prepared to give this, even though Peter had been welcomed into their home as a fellow Christian and respected missionary. Like any devoted father, Charles Field was reluctant to see his daughter, who was small and delicate, give up a comfortable existence for the precarious life of a missionary's wife.

The young couple were very persuasive, however. By March 15, they had come up with a compromise. Peter would return to Canada and make arrangements to provide for Eliza's financial security. If the arrangements met with Field's approval, the wedding could proceed. Peter left a few weeks later.

While they were apart, Eliza visited a friend to learn the basics of cooking, sewing, and knitting. Just as everything seemed to be falling into place, however, Field withdrew his permission.

Perhaps his earlier agreement had been a ploy to separate Peter and Eliza in hopes that the young woman would reconsider. But Peter's biographer, Donald B. Smith, suggests another reason: Field had just learned about the behaviour of Peter's father.

Augustus Jones was well-known in Ontario frontier society. He had surveyed vast tracts of the colony, amassing large landholdings in the process. But his liaisons with Aboriginal women had scandalized other European settlers. Jones had eventually left Peter's mother and married an Iroquois woman from the Six Nations. As far as Eliza's father was concerned, these highly irregular domestic arrangements reflected badly on Peter's character.

Fortunately, two prominent Methodists came to the rescue. Reverend Robert Alder, superintendent of Wesleyan Methodist missions, and Egerton Ryerson, editor of the *Christian Guardian*, an influential Methodist newspaper, had nothing but praise for the young man. Regardless of his father's failings — and Jones, they pointed out, had reformed as he aged — Peter was above reproach. Reluctantly, Field gave in.

When the couple had been separated for more than a year, Peter sent word that he would be unable to make the trip to England. Instead, he asked Eliza to meet him in New York City, where they would be married.

Field was enraged. All his suspicions about Peter resurfaced. Once more, Ryerson intervened, persuading Field to allow him to escort Eliza to New York.

Ryerson and Eliza reached New York on September 4, and Peter arrived four days later. It was a Sunday, and what more auspicious day could there be for the wedding of a couple who planned to devote their lives to the service of God? The two were married that evening.

The sweetness of their reunion after such a long separation and so many trials was marred by public opinion. The comments of family and friends were nothing compared to the opinions expressed after their marriage. A New York newspaper compared Eliza to Desdemona, the Shakespearean character murdered by Othello, her black husband. "We longed to interpose and rescue her," the reporter lamented. Canadian newspapers reprinted the story, adding their own embellishments. With a few notable exceptions, most claimed to be horrified by the interracial marriage.

Eliza and Peter drew attention almost everywhere they went. "My peculiar situation in connection with my dear husband excites much unpleasant curiosity,"

Eliza wrote. "I feel myself gazed on wherever I move." Nevertheless, she soon settled into her new home, a small cabin on the Credit Reserve.

Eliza's life in Canada was frequently difficult. She was often ill, and by 1836, she had been pregnant four times and lost four babies, although she and Peter eventually produced four healthy children. Along with raising a family, they were deeply absorbed in their missionary work.

In 1841, Peter was posted to the Muncey Mission, near London, and eight years later, he was transferred to the Brantford area. During this time, his health deteriorated, and in 1856, he died at the age of 52.

Eliza eventually remarried, although it was not a happy union, and she eventually left her husband to live alone. No one could replace her beloved Peter. As their dear friend Ryerson observed, "I question whether a happier marriage than theirs, on both sides, was ever experienced — truly in life they were of one heart."

Though Eliza Field left her home and comfortable life to be with the man she loved, Thomas Ashburnham had no thought of romance when he moved to Canada from England. The fifth son of the fourth Earl of Ashburnham, Tom was born in 1855, and after leaving Trinity College, had served with the Queen's Own Hussars in South

Africa, Egypt, Ireland, and India. Decorated by Queen Victoria, the khedive of Egypt and the sultan of Turkey for his bravery in the Egyptian Rebellion of 1882, he retired from the army just before 1900.

With a military pension and a generous allowance from his family, Tom did not need to work. He spent most of his time drinking and gambling, both of which he enjoyed to excess. As a result, his family decided to send him overseas, where his escapades could be more easily overlooked.

Tom had visited most other parts of the British Empire, so Canada was an appropriate choice. Two of his older brothers had already visited the country, and his cousin, Lord Aberdeen, had served as governor general. The retired soldier arrived and drifted from city to city before settling in at Windsor Hall, the newest and most luxurious hotel in Fredericton, New Brunswick.

Tom's place of residence may have changed, but his habits had not. Every evening, cane in hand, he strolled to the Fredericton City Club. As the evening progressed, he usually visited several other drinking establishments. By the time he was ready to return to Windsor Hall, he was no longer inclined to walk. Invariably, he picked up the nearest telephone and asked the night operator to ring the livery stable for a horse and carriage to take him back to the hotel.

Invariably, the same telephone operator answered his call.

When the New Brunswick Telephone Company was established in 1888, one of the first night operators was Maria Elizabeth Anderson, the daughter of a former city alderman. Rye, as she was known, was one of the new breed of women determined to make their own way in the world. Company subscribers soon became familiar with her pleasant voice and soft laughter.

Gradually, the friendly telephone operator and the inebriated former soldier moved from businesslike conversations to prolonged chats, then face-to-face meetings. Although Rye was over 40, she was small, lively, and attractive. Tom began spending as much time as he could in her company. Eventually, they came to an understanding, and in the spring of 1903, he went home to tell his family that he intended to marry.

The Ashburnhams were not enthusiastic about the match, but unable to stop it, they put up a united front. Discreet notices of the forthcoming union appeared in British papers. These were in marked contrast to headline that blazed from the *Boston Herald* on June 10: Captain the Honourable Thomas Ashburnham Marries Telephone Girl at Fredericton.

When the couple married in St. Ann's Parish Church, the *Fredericton Gleaner* reported the ceremony in detail. The radiant bride carried white roses and wore an elaborate dress that she had helped make herself. At the altar, the couple stood alone on a robe of silver jackal skin. On four state occasions, Queen Victoria had stood on the same robe. After the ceremony and a reception at Rye's home, the two left for a honeymoon in the Saint John Valley.

When they returned, they lived at 163 and 165 Brunswick Street, a block from Rye's childhood home. Her husband had purchased both houses and arranged to have them joined. Rye used the lower house, 165, for her personal quarters, while her husband used the upper house. Tom often joked, "Whenever I want to see my wife, I have to go next door."

Marriage brought important changes to their lives. Rye quit her job, and Tom stopped visiting taverns. Instead, they concentrated on entertaining Fredericton society with lavish teas and dinners. They also devoted many hours to philanthropic work.

They lived in this fashion for nearly a decade, until January 1913, when a telegram from England changed their lives. Tom's elder brother had died. His only child, a daughter, was ineligible to inherit the title, and all other male members of the family had succumbed to lung ailments.

The black sheep of the family became the next

earl, making his wife, the retired telephone operator, the right honourable the Countess of Ashburnham, the Viscountess of St. Asaph, and the Baroness Ashburnham.

The couple moved to England, where they seemed prepared to make their home. Rye was not completely accepted in aristocratic circles, however, and was never presented at court. What's more, war clouds were gathering over Europe, and Sussex was near the continent. It would be hardest hit if an invasion materialized. On June 20, 1914, the couple sailed from Liverpool aboard the *Megantic*. They were accompanied by three servants and numerous family heirlooms and works of art.

Life continued as it had before Tom inherited the title, although on a slightly grander scale. But Rye never forgot her humble origins. On at least one occasion, she answered the door wearing carpet slippers, explaining to her guests that her feet heart. Some wit promptly dubbed her "the carpet-slipper countess."

Tom died in 1924 after contracting pneumonia on a rare voyage home to England. He was the last of a line extending back to the time of the Norman Conquest, and his widow saw him buried in the family vault. Then she settled his affairs and returned to Fredericton, where she continued her charitable work until her own death in 1938.

Chapter 4
Unrequited Love

When a man loves a woman — or a woman loves a man — he or she hopes the affection is returned. But life does not always work out as expected. Feelings fade, other commitments intervene, and what might have been a grand passion becomes a bittersweet memory.

Admiral Horatio Nelson was a brilliant British naval hero, whose exploits are well documented. When attention turns to his private life, it usually focuses on his love affair with Lady Emma Hamilton, another man's wife. Emma bore Horatio two daughters and flattered him ceaselessly, filling her house with mementoes of the honours he had won and souvenirs of his naval battles. Although critics observed that Emma was often vulgar, self-indulgent, and lacking in discretion, Horatio ignored his own wife's pleas to return home and devoted his attention to Emma from late 1799 until his death at Trafalgar in October 1805.

Though Horatio's affair with Emma is one of the more famous love stories of history, neither Emma nor his wife was the admiral's first love. This honour belonged to a young Canadian woman who barely acknowledged his existence. Had Horatio followed his heart, he might have abandoned his naval career to be near her.

In September 1781, Horatio was captain of the *Albemarle,* a ship on convoy duty in the Atlantic. The American Revolution was raging, and the crew had not had fresh food since leaving England in April. Many were beginning to suffer from scurvy. To take on fresh provisions and find medical help for those who were ill, Horatio put into port at Quebec and gave the crew a month's leave.

The leave was a rare break from duty for the 24-year-old naval officer. For the first time in his life, he was unconfined by family or naval restrictions, and he plunged into the social season that had just started in the colonial town.

As a British naval officer, albeit a relatively unimportant one, the young man was a welcome guest at receptions, balls, and teas, where he met many eligible young women. Among them was Mary Simpson, daughter of the provost marshal of the Quebec garrison. At 16, Mary was already one of the most popular young women in town, and Horatio fell madly in love with her.

Biographers have suggested this was his first romantic encounter. Unlike most sailors, Horatio had had little or no experience with women. Raised in a country vicarage, he had spent his teen years and early adulthood carrying out his naval duties. In Quebec, the rare combination of free time, distance from home, and a pretty face proved irresistible.

Unfortunately, Mary did not return his affection. He was an insignificant naval officer, and the spoiled young woman hoped to marry someone wealthy and powerful. Mary had her pick of men, although Horatio apparently chose to ignore this.

As his leave drew to an end, Horatio received orders to escort troop transports to New York. He confided to a friend, Alexander Davison, that he intended to resign his commission and ask Mary to marry him. Davison was horrified. Ten years older than Horatio, he was far more worldly wise than his friend. He also knew Mary's father and may have discussed Mary's feelings about Horatio with him. With some difficulty, Davison persuaded his friend not to abandon his duty, especially during war. When the *Albemarle* sailed from Quebec, Horatio sailed with her — and into history.

Though Horatio Nelson may have flirted with the idea of abandoning duty and his career for the sake of love, another famous Briton flatly refused to do this. Or so an Ontario legend claims.

Florence Nightingale was the pretty, intelligent daughter of a wealthy landowner. As a young woman, she had her share of boyfriends, among them her cousin, John Smithurst. Born in Lea, Derbyshire, England, in September 1807, John was a sturdy, serious fellow who found work as a merchant's assistant in London. He was also deeply — and hopelessly — in love with his cousin Florence. Although he was neither as handsome nor as wealthy as his rivals, John proposed marriage. Few were surprised when Florence turned him down.

The rejection, however, had more to do with Florence's personality than her love interests. Restless and imaginative, she was already struggling against Victorian conventions that assumed that she would become a wife and mother.

John was deeply wounded by her rejection. "I asked

Florence what I was to do since she could not marry me, and she replied, 'John, I would like you to be a missionary to the Indians in North America.'"

He followed her advice. In 1839, he was ordained a clerk in Holy Orders and, shortly afterwards, sailed for Canada as a representative of the Church Missionary Society. His first posting was as chaplain at the Hudson's Bay Company post in Fort Garry, now Winnipeg. On his arrival, he learned that the Aboriginal people had built a house for him in their village, and he chose to live among them. For 12 years, he ministered to both settlers and Aboriginal people, braving many hardships to carry out his work.

In 1851, John returned to England. Always taciturn, he said little about the reason for his trip, but friends suspected that his purpose was to propose to Florence again. If he did, he was rejected once again.

Legend suggests that Florence, who had already refused several other marriage proposals, loved John but could not marry him because of parental opposition. Whatever the truth, John returned to Canada in 1852 and became rector of St. John's Church in Elora, Canada West.

Meanwhile, Florence finally found a calling of her own. Soon after John's departure, she enrolled in nursing school in Germany, an action that horrified her parents and friends. At this time, the typical hospital nurse was usually untrained and often either a thief or a prostitute — and frequently both. These women preyed on patients, doing little to alleviate their suffering.

Florence chose to disregard the opposition to her decision and completed her studies in time to lead a contingent of British nurses to the front lines during the Crimean War.

In Canada, John eagerly pounced upon every snippet of news about the progress of the war, including reports of the brave and dedicated "Lady with the Lamp." Was Florence's deep involvement in nursing after his departure from England mere coincidence? Or had John challenged her, just as she had challenged him, to throw herself into some kind of altruistic service?

No one knows for certain, but there are tantalizing hints, including a silver communion service that was sent to John in Elora. The vessels were presented on behalf of a mysterious donor. On the paten — the shallow plate used to hold the communion wafer — is this inscription: To Reverend John Smithurst, a very dear friend, in grateful recognition of his many kindnesses, A.D. 1852.

According to John, Florence was the "dear friend." His version of events found its way into oral tradition, and eventually, the story of the romance between the Canadian missionary and the nursing pioneer was written down.

Experts on Florence Nightingale's life claim that there is no truth to the story — and no trace of a cousin named John Smithurst in her family tree. Did John lie to make himself seem important to his parishioners? Or did the romance really happen, with Florence and John choosing not to record events that were too painful to discuss? No one may ever know for sure.

Although love is often compared to madness, most lovers manage to retain a grip on reality. But there are many exceptions, including one young woman who was boarding with a Halifax family in 1863.

Toward the end of that year, a French cook employed by General Sir Charles Hastings Doyle visited the Saunders family on Sackville Street in Halifax. Mr. Saunders was a bank employee who often helped out at banquets and special dinners, and the cook wanted his assistance. As he was explaining his errand to Mrs. Saunders, an envelope on a table caught his eye.

"Who in this house is writing to Victor Hugo?" he asked.

Mrs. Saunders replied that the letter had been written by their boarder, Miss Llewly.

"Don't you know who Victor Hugo is?" the cook asked.

Mrs. Saunders had no idea, but by the time the cook left, she had been informed that Victor Hugo was one of France's greatest writers. The news was one more perplexing bit of information about the mysterious young woman who had lived with the family since late summer. As she carefully copied the address, Mrs. Saunders made up her mind to write to France to find out about the young woman and to explain the unusual circumstances in which she was living.

Mrs. Saunders believed that Victor Hugo must be a friend or relative of Miss Llewly, for despite her name, the young woman spoke English with a heavy French accent. In August, she had arrived in Halifax from New York and taken a room at the Hotel Halifax. Finding these accommodations too expensive, she had arranged to board with the Saunders family.

Tall, dark-haired, and attractive, Miss Llewly was obviously a woman of good social standing and above-average education. Her manners were exquisite, and Mrs. Saunders had noticed that her wardrobe contained many expensive garments, though some had become rather shabby. The landlady believed that the young woman was a rich lady who had fallen on hard times.

But there was even more to the mysterious Miss Llewly. She behaved very oddly at times. When the family had moved from Barrington to Sackville Street, she had asked to go along and had insisted on furnishing her room herself. Although buying furniture seemed to indicate an interest in domesticity, the boarder seemed incapable of keeping the room tidy. Papers were spread everywhere, yet she ignored the mess. She also seemed oblivious to the absence of a fireplace and the fact that she was not suitably dressed for a winter on the shores of the North Atlantic. She bought her food at the local market but seemed to eat nothing but bread, butter, and vegetables, washed down with cups of tea or chocolate. Aside from the occasional outing to buy writing paper or to walk near the garrison where British troops were stationed, Miss Llewly rarely went out and seemed to have few friends.

There was one notable exception, but whether he could be called a friend was debatable. Soon after her arrival in town, Miss Llewly told the manager of the Hotel Halifax that she was looking for a cousin, a soldier named Pinson, who was stationed in Halifax. A lawyer soon found the man for her, and he had come to call a few times.

It was obvious that Miss Llewly was deeply in love with this man. Although he had visited perhaps half a dozen times and written the occasional letter, Miss Llewly plunged into melancholy whenever they were out of contact. And although she never initiated a conversation about him, if her landlord worked at a banquet where the soldier was present, the young woman's face shone with interest as she peppered Saunders with questions. How was he dressed? Who was he with? What had he said?

Miss Llewly seemed to be wrapped up in the soldier, although the Saunderses suspected that her affection was not returned. After each of his calls, their roomer was short of cash, and the couple concluded that she was giving her lover what little money she had.

Mrs. Saunders outlined her observations and concerns in the letter to France. Before the end of the year, she had received a reply from François-Victor Hugo, the writer's son. "Miss Llewly" was his sister Adèle, who had left the family home to follow the man she loved.

Adèle Hugo was born on July 28, 1830, the fifth child of Victor and Adèle Hugo. Her childhood was generally happy — until September 1843, when her elder sister Leopoldine and her husband of eight months were drowned in a boating accident. Devastated, Adèle was haunted by the deaths for many years.

By 1848, she seemed to be coping with her grief. Then another upheaval threatened the family. Her father and brothers became involved in the revolution that swept France that year (and which Victor Hugo described in *Les Misérables*). Adèle's brothers were thrown into jail for their anti-government writings, and by December, her father had fled to Belgium. At an age when she should have been joining the social whirl of Paris, Adèle was confined to the family home, probably spied upon by government agents and shunned by friends worried about their own safety.

At her mother's urging, Adèle studied English, for Mme Hugo foresaw the possibility of exile to England. Finally, when Charles and François-Victor were released in 1852, the family moved to the Channel Island of Jersey, and later to Guernsey, where they purchased a house.

After months of separation, the reunion of the Hugo family was joyous. Gradually, though, the novelty of being together in a new place wore off. Adèle amused herself by playing the piano, which she did exceptionally well, and by continuing the journal she had started several years earlier. But aside from her brothers and Auguste Vacquerie, her dead sister's brother-in-law, there were few young people with whom she could socialize.

Still, as a pretty young woman who would receive a sizable fortune on her marriage, Adèle attracted her share of suitors. At 16, she had fallen in love with Auguste, but the young man's position as Hugo's foster son complicated the romance. In the view of many, he was more like a brother than a suitor.

Meanwhile, other men vied for Adèle's affections. At least five proposed, but she rejected them all, countering criticism with the comment that she could not be blamed for her reluctance to change a name as prestigious as Hugo. Her refusal involved more than family pride, however. She wanted to be appreciated for her creative accomplishments — her writing and her musical ability — rather than for her looks or domestic skills. More important, after 1854, Adèle could not seriously consider any marriage proposal, for she had fallen passionately and irrevocably in love with Lieutenant Albert Andrew Pinson.

Little is known about Albert's life, and much of that may have been garbled by Adèle's confusing accounts. When the couple first met, the tall, elegantly dressed Englishman was serving with the Yorkshire Militia on Jersey. He had been well educated and spoke French beautifully. There, his good points ended. Albert was a spendthrift, who had been forced to choose between joining the army and going to debtor's prison. He learned little from his mistakes. For the rest of his life, gambling on horses and dressing expensively kept him permanently short of cash.

Yet something about him attracted Adèle. Perhaps it was his air of sophistication. He was reputedly several years older than she, although he used liberal applications of hair dye and rouge to maintain a youthful appearance. Perhaps Adèle was also attracted by the aristocratic haughtiness that led his military comrades to nickname him "the Count." In the summer of 1854, when Albert spent several months on Jersey, he was a guest at the Hugo house no fewer than six times.

Early on, Adèle's parents suspected that Albert was not the kind of man they wanted as a son-in-law. Though they hoped their daughter would choose one of the other young men who visited, she resisted. She wanted to marry Albert, no one else. As for Albert, if he had ever promised marriage, he changed his mind. By late 1860, he was trying to end the relationship.

One of his excuses for delaying the marriage was his lack of money. "That's not a reason," Adèle complained to her journal. The income she would receive from her father after her marriage could support them both. Albert had other excuses, however. He told her that he would be labelled a coward if he resigned from the army. Adèle suggested that he resign anyway, then use her dowry to buy a better commission and seek a posting in one of the empire's trouble spots. After this, there could be no suggestion of cowardice. Still, her lieutenant hesitated.

In February 1861, Adèle took action after her

mother left for a Paris vacation. Adèle was supposed to follow. Instead, she and her servant, Rosalie, went to the Isle of Wight, about 100 kilometres from Aldershot, where Albert was stationed. Only after she had rented a house of her own did Adèle contact her family to tell them where she was.

After a swift exchange of angry, excited letters, Adèle returned home in disgrace. Her family believed that the escapade not only suggested moral weakness, but also reduced Adèle's chances of making a suitable marriage. They watched her carefully. For several months, Adèle could not walk by herself or go to a shop alone.

As her parents stepped up their efforts to find their daughter a husband, Adèle became more determined to have her own way. She would break free, she vowed in her diary. But first, she tried to persuade her family to accept Albert. Because her father would not discuss the matter, Adèle wrote him a letter in the spring of 1863. She explained that she and the lieutenant had been in contact, that she loved him, and that she wished to marry him. She also explained Albert's precarious financial situation. If Hugo bothered to reply, there is no trace of his response. Perhaps his silence goaded Adèle to plan another escape.

Adèle arranged to take a trip with a friend and her two children. They were supposed to take the ferry to

Weymouth, then proceed to Paris, where Adèle's mother was waiting. Instead, Adèle went to visit another friend in England and wrote to her family from there. François-Victor, the brother who had always been closest to Adèle, was convinced that this was another trick. His sister soon confirmed his suspicions.

In an anguished letter, she explained that "Mr. P." could not be expected to resign his commission to marry her, as this would jeopardize his future. Because she had already waited nine years and could bear to wait no longer, she would follow him to Malta. The family could tell people that she had been staying with friends in England and had married there.

Adèle was either uncertain of Albert's whereabouts, or she was deliberately trying to throw her family off track. Instead of sailing for Malta, she boarded the *Great Eastern* for New York, where she caught a mail boat to Halifax. Albert's regiment had been posted there to provide additional security in the tense days of the American Civil War.

Adèle's family knew nothing of her whereabouts until Mrs. Saunders made contact. Then Adèle began writing letters home. Meanwhile, her landlady kept François-Victor informed of his sister's activities. At his request, Adèle was provided with a stove for her room, nourishing meals, and clothing more suited to the

Canadian climate.

Adèle stayed with the Saunderses for about 18 months. When a nearby building caught fire, she began to worry about the safety of her manuscripts and moved again, finally settling with the family of Robert Motton, a well-known Halifax lawyer. Again, François-Victor requested help in caring for his sister, and the Mottons obliged.

More than most Haligonians, Motton understood the reason for Adèle's eccentricities, for he was one of two lawyers to whom she revealed details of her ill-fated romance. Normally secretive, Adèle felt compelled to tell her story after learning of Albert's engagement to Agnes Johnstone, the daughter of Nova Scotia's former premier. When the engagement was announced, Adèle called on a lawyer named Lenoir. Dissatisfied with his advice, she sought a second opinion from Motton.

The story she told was a complicated blend of fact and fantasy. She said that Albert was the son of an Anglican clergyman, who opposed their liaison for religious reasons. Nevertheless, they had become engaged and signed a marriage contract. As soon as this was done, Adèle's father began pressuring Albert to marry her. Then Albert left for England. When military duties made it impossible for him to return, he sent for Adèle, promising that they would be married publicly in an

Anglican church. Adèle's family wanted a marriage on Guernsey, but after she made a scene, her mother agreed to accompany her to England for the ceremony. When they got there, they were astounded to find that Albert had left for Halifax with his regiment.

Adèle said that she was confused, unsure whether Albert had deliberately abandoned her or simply been forced to obey orders. To find out, she decided to follow him and persuaded her parents to support her decision. When she arrived in Halifax, she contacted Albert, who swore he loved her but said he could not marry without his father's consent. His engagement to Agnes Johnstone complicated matters, but Adèle said that the marriage contract made her Albert's wife in the eyes of God.

Although his correspondence with the Hugo family must have persuaded Motton that Adèle was not telling the whole truth, he relayed her story to Agnes Johnstone's father. Agnes's engagement to Albert ended abruptly, and the young woman was sent to England for a long visit. She never married.

Albert was furious and refused to have anything to do with Adèle. After this, her behaviour became increasingly eccentric; she often stayed up all night, pacing her room. Meanwhile, her parents had issued an ultimatum: marry or come home.

Somehow, Adèle managed to convince her family

that she had married Albert. Although François-Victor remained sceptical, he yielded to his father's decision to behave as though the marriage had indeed occurred. On October 9, 1863, Adèle's engagement was announced in the Guernsey newspapers. Eight days later, the marriage notice appeared, and François-Victor was instructed to place additional announcements in other English newspapers. At the very least, he reasoned, Albert would be cornered into marrying Adèle if he had not already done so.

When his mother expressed doubts of her own, François-Victor suggested that Adèle had not described the ceremony because she had been married in the Anglican church and did not wish to upset her parents. Privately, he wrote to Albert asking for a copy of the marriage certificate.

Eventually, Albert sent a chilly response, telling François-Victor that he had no intention of marrying Adèle and had been surprised to read that Victor Hugo had given him the "unsolicited honour" of his daughter's hand. He said that he had seen Adèle after her arrival in Halifax; she had told him she was travelling with a friend and would be leaving soon but had found numerous excuses to delay her departure. Albert also claimed that he had written a letter denying any intention of marriage and had given it to Adèle to mail to her family. After waiting more than two months for a reply, he had become convinced that she had destroyed the letter.

Whether he was acting from selfish motives or real concern for Adèle, Albert warned François-Victor that his sister must return home as soon as possible. Her living quarters were far from suitable, he said, and the ever-present possibility of encounters with soldiers made Halifax dangerous for unescorted women.

By November 11, François-Victor had informed his father that Adèle was not married. Worse, the announcement Hugo had hoped would silence gossip was not working. Albert's family had publicly denied the liaison, and there was nothing left to do but persuade Adèle to return home.

This was not easy. Adèle came up with one excuse after another, promising to come home and requesting money for the fare, then spending it on stationery or gifts for Albert. Her family finally resigned themselves to the fact that Adèle would come home only when Albert's regiment returned to England.

In the meantime, Adèle remained convinced that she could persuade Albert to marry her. At one point, she thought of hiring a hypnotist to help. For 5,000 francs — a sizable sum — the hypnotist would cast a spell on Albert and provide a clergyman and two witnesses to see that the wedding was carried out. Though nothing came of the plan, it drove home the fact that Adèle's obsession had pushed her beyond the bounds of reason. Still, her family continued to nurse the slim hope that she would return on her own and sent money whenever she requested it.

In 1866, Adèle finally left Halifax, but not to go home. Albert's regiment had been posted to Barbados. Adèle knew that officers were often granted leave between postings, and when news of the transfer became public, she hired a coach to take her to the dock whenever a ship was due to leave for Liverpool. These efforts to catch a glimpse of Albert were in vain. He left for Barbados without visiting England.

Adèle soon followed — and became a familiar figure on the tropical island. At first, no one knew who she was. Eventually, however, her name was linked to that of Albert, who had earned a reputation as a gambler, an enthusiastic racing fan, and a not-altogether-honest individual.

Traces of Adèle's beauty and solid upbringing remained, and the hint of a secret tragedy evoked a certain sympathy among Barbadians. Nevertheless, she had become an eccentric, who seldom talked to anyone. Every day, early in the morning and at night, she walked about, dressed in silks, heavy fabrics, and occasionally, furs, clothing completely unsuitable for the hot climate. Despite this odd behaviour, Adèle continued to correspond with her family until her mother's death in August 1868. After that, there was very little communication, although she continued to request money, and her father continued to send it.

In 1872, Hugo hired Mme Céline Alvarez Baa, a Barbadian who had nursed Adèle during an illness, to bring his daughter back to France. There, Adèle was confined to an asylum. Although convinced that she heard voices, she was normally calm and gentle and recognized her family when they visited.

Sadly, their visits became less and less frequent. Her mother and her brother Charles had died while she was away; in 1873, François-Victor died; and her father died in 1885. Adèle lived for another 30 years, tending the garden, playing music, and wrapping herself in memories of a love beyond all reason.

Chapter 5
Passionate Politicians

Canadian politicians have a reputation for being a little dull. When it comes to romance, however, some of the country's most famous leaders have also been leading lovers.

In 1870, Ontario premier John Sandfield Macdonald celebrated his 30th wedding anniversary. Though government business kept Ontario's first premier from spending the day with his wife in Cornwall, he found time to write a letter in which he expressed appreciation for her "excellent qualities" and "varied accomplishments," as well as for her patient tolerance of his "peculiarities of temper."

Awkward about expressing emotions, Macdonald

didn't mention love. Yet more than 30 years earlier, he had risked life, limb, and the possibility of an international diplomatic incident to elope with his beloved.

Born to Scots immigrants in St. Raphael West, Glengarry County, Upper Canada, on December 12, 1812, John was an independent and often unruly youngster. After leaving school at 16, he worked as a clerk in a general store and in a post office. Eventually, he decided to study law and was articled to Archibald McLean, the leading Tory lawyer in Cornwall. McLean used his considerable influence to obtain a military commission for the young man. As a result, John became a royal messenger, carrying dispatches between the lieutenant-governor of Upper Canada in Toronto and the British minister in Washington.

At the time, relations between British North America and the United States were strained. The recent rebellion in the Canadian colonies had sparked Yankee hopes of driving the British from the continent. Rebels, including leader William Lyon Mackenzie, had fled to the U.S., where some planned further attacks on Canada. Consequently, Macdonald's missions were sometimes dangerous.

In 1838, travelling with an armed guard, he stopped at Saratoga Springs, New York. The spa was a fashionable resort where wealthy Americans gathered,

John Sandfield Macdonald

and the arrival of a British-Canadian contingent attracted attention. During his brief stay, John met Marie Christine Waggaman, an 18-year-old Louisiana Creole who was on vacation with her father and two sisters.

Christine was a charming southern belle who had grown up speaking French on Avondale, the family's sugar plantation. Like John, she was a Roman Catholic, and she was immediately attracted to the tall, slim royal

Christine Waggaman Macdonald

messenger with the deep grey eyes and thick, wavy hair. In his previous travels, Macdonald had carried on flirtations with several young women. This time, his relationship went beyond flirtation. He and Christine fell in love.

It wasn't long before her father heard of their relationship. George Augustus Waggaman, who had served as a judge and a state senator, was not pleased. In his view, the young royal messenger was beneath notice.

Instead, he favoured a marriage between Christine and Teakle Wallis, a prominent Baltimore lawyer.

Because Christine was attending a private finishing school in Baltimore, it seemed likely that she would quickly forget about her flirtation with the handsome Canadian and concentrate on Wallis. Waggaman, however, had not reckoned with John's determination. Baltimore was near Washington, D.C., and pretending to be a relative, the young man visited Christine's school whenever he could.

The clandestine meetings were risky. As a royal messenger, John was supposed to be above reproach, and word of a secret courtship could embarrass his government. On a more personal level, the young man might be challenged to a duel by Christine's father. Waggaman was certainly capable of resorting to pistols to defend an insult to his honour: he was destined to be killed in a duel in 1843.

The lovers were lucky. They weren't found out, and their secret meetings continued until 1840, when Macdonald was called to the bar. By then, it was too late for family interference. When John paid his final visit to the school, Christine climbed over the garden wall to meet him, and they ran away to be married in New York.

Christine's father never quite forgave her, and he died too soon to see how well the marriage turned out.

Not only did the young royal messenger enjoy a successful career in law and public life, but the marriage was a happy one, lasting until John's death in June 1872.

When she climbed the garden wall, Christine Waggaman had no idea that her lover was destined to be the first premier of Ontario. But another woman who fell in love with another John Macdonald was fully aware of her beloved's political ambitions.

In late 1866, John Alexander Macdonald was in London, England, putting the final touches on arrangements that would lead to Canadian confederation. While walking along Bond street one day, the future prime minister bumped into an old friend, Agnes Bernard.

They had once been more than friends. Born in Spanish Town, Jamaica, in 1836, Agnes was the daughter of a politician. With her brother Hewitt and widowed mother, she had moved to Barrie, Ontario, in about 1856. Shortly after the family's arrival, John, who was then attorney general of the Province of Canada, saw Agnes and her brother in a Toronto dining room. "I thought you both very tall, very much alike, and that you had fine eyes, " he said later. Although he asked a companion about them, his friend could tell him only that the family had settled near Lake Simcoe.

That same year, John's first wife, Isabella, had died.

Although the 41-year-old politician had been a deeply devoted husband, Isabella's death after more than 10 years of sickness came as something of a relief. Finally, he was free to concentrate on his political career.

It soon became apparent that he could probably remarry any time he wanted to. Though far from handsome, John was a charming man who had always enjoyed a certain popularity with women. As his political power increased, he became the most eligible bachelor in the country.

Agnes, of course, had heard about him soon after she arrived in Canada. She heard even more when Hewitt went to work in the attorney general's office. Not only did her brother become Macdonald's assistant, but he also shared bachelor quarters with him from time to time.

The first time Agnes actually saw John was at a concert in 1859. When Hewitt pointed him out, he was sitting at the front of the balcony surrounded by several women. "I remember distinctly how he looked," she wrote later, "a forcible, yet changeful face, with such a mixture of strength and vivacity, and his busy, dark, peculiar hair as he leaned on his elbows and looked down."

Later that year, John called at the Bernard residence, explaining to Mrs. Bernard that he liked her son so much that he thought he should make her acquaintance as well.

Whether he was actually looking for an introduction

to Agnes is unknown, but the two became close friends in the ensuing months. The Canadian capital, which moved to a new city every so often, was located in Quebec City at the time. There was plenty to do, especially in the winter, when skating, tobogganing, and other outdoor sports were very fashionable. There were also various forms of indoor entertainment, including balls and concerts. On Valentine's Day, Agnes was one of 800 guests invited to a ball hosted by the attorney general.

Like John, Agnes was intelligent and strong-willed. She was also well educated and an excellent conversationalist. But she had a puritanical streak, disapproving of cards, gambling, and excessive drinking — and Macdonald's tendency to drink excessively was common knowledge.

Nevertheless, the two were attracted, and John may have proposed. Agnes apparently decided not to risk marriage to a heavy drinker and turned him down. Then, in 1865, the Bernards moved to London, England.

The move may have been motivated by a desire to lead a more urbane lifestyle. Even Montreal, arguably Canada's most sophisticated city at the time, hardly rivalled the British capital. And Ottawa, chosen as the capital of the soon-to-be-created Dominion of Canada, was little more than a lumber town, short on accommodations and amenities. In any event, Agnes and her mother left Canada — and that might have been the last John ever heard of them.

The chance encounter in Bond Street offered Agnes and John a chance to renew their friendship. He had apparently cut back on his drinking, a situation Agnes would have found gratifying. But this alone might not have been enough to persuade her to marry him if fate hadn't intervened.

Late on the night of December 12, John returned to his hotel room. He climbed into bed, gathered his newspapers, and started to catch up on the news of the day by candlelight. The next thing he knew, he was waking to a sensation of incredible heat. The bed curtains and blankets were on fire.

Pulling down the curtains, he doused them with water from a nearby pitcher. Then he roused two of his colleagues in adjoining rooms, and together, they battled the flames. Only after they had brought the fire under control did Macdonald realize that he had singed his head and hands and that his shoulder was badly burned. At first, he thought the injuries were minor. But a week later, he was forced to see a doctor, who ordered immediate bed rest.

The near-fatal fire probably helped Agnes make up her mind. The couple became engaged.

On February 16, 1867, Susan Agnes Bernard and

John Alexander Macdonald were married at St. George's Church in Hanover Square. Wearing white satin and Brussels lace, Agnes was attended by four bridesmaids dressed in blue and pink crepe. All four were daughters of Canadian delegates to the London Conference. After the ceremony, the newlyweds and their guests adjourned to John's hotel for a lavish wedding breakfast.

The pair sandwiched a quick honeymoon between the first and second readings of the British North America bill, then returned to Ottawa in the spring. There, Agnes found herself immersed in the official duties of a prime minister's wife. She also discovered that many people tried to influence John through her, a practice she quickly discouraged. As she wrote to one friend, "If I interfere in any sort of way he will be annoyed, and more, he will be 'disinclined', I know him so well." Yet she had opinions on many subjects and probably discussed politics with her husband regularly.

The one heartbreak of the couple's married life was the birth of their daughter Mary, who was severely handicapped. Aside from that tragedy, Agnes found her union very satisfactory, and those who knew the prime minister realized how good she was for him. She often sat in the visitors' gallery during parliamentary debates, and if the sessions ran late, she was usually there to make sure her husband bundled up against the weather and went directly home. She was, in the words of MP John Charlton, Macdonald's "good angel."

Like many politicians' wives, Agnes Macdonald played a supporting role in her husband's career. Sometimes, however, the women behind successful politicians were not their wives, but their mistresses.

One man whose success can be attributed directly to the influence of a mistress was Prime Minister Wilfrid Laurier. Without the shrewd advice of Emilie Lavergne, Laurier might never have been more than a well-to-do Quebec lawyer with an interest in politics.

Emilie was nearly 30 and had recently returned from a visit to France and England when she walked across the lawn at a garden party and into Wilfrid's life. By this time, Wilfrid had been practising law in Arthabaskaville, in Quebec's Eastern Townships, for nearly a decade. During much of that time, he had been married to the former Zöe Lafontaine.

The future prime minister had met his wife when, as a law student at McGill University in Montreal, he had boarded in the house of Dr. Séraphin Gauthier, Zöe's foster father. Wilfrid, who liked women and found it impossible not to flirt with them, became fond of the shy young music teacher. When he moved to the Eastern Townships in 1866, however, the relationship deteriorated, and Zöe eventually became engaged to a Montreal doctor.

Nearly two years after they parted, Wilfrid received an urgent telegram from Gauthier. Responding to the summons, he took the first train to Montreal and hurried to his former boarding house. There, after the doctor had assured himself that Wilfrid's persistent cough was caused by chronic bronchitis and not tuberculosis, a much more serious disease, Gauthier told him that Zöe had burst into tears the day before, insisting that she would marry Wilfrid Laurier or no one.

That evening, Wilfrid and Zöe were married in the Gauthiers' house. Almost as soon as the ceremony was over, the bridegroom hopped on a train to keep a court date in Arthabaskaville.

This was a rocky beginning to a marriage that would last several decades. More misfortune followed. The Lauriers never had children. Worse, Zöe was uninterested in politics during the early years of Wilfrid's career, and she lacked both the personality and the ambition that might have made her an asset to her husband.

Emilie Barthe was cut from a different cloth. Witty, ambitious, intelligent, and well-informed, she was immediately attracted by the young lawyer whose laziness threatened to eclipse his charm and brilliance. Within weeks, she had married Wilfrid's partner, Joseph Lavergne.

At first, the small town of Arthabaskaville was scandalized by the arrangement. Few doubted that it was anything but a marriage of convenience for both Emilie and Wilfrid. Nearly every day, either in the late morning or late afternoon, Wilfrid would rise from his desk in the office and remark to his partner, "Joseph, if you will permit it, I am going to chat with your wife." Joseph, it seemed, always permitted.

In later years, Emilie described to her nephew the Wilfrid Laurier she had known in those days. He was, she recalled, "the little greenhorn," with scant knowledge of etiquette and an even scantier sense of style, both of which were essential for a successful politician. Emilie became his image consultant, and Wilfrid happily submitted to her tutelage.

A devout Anglophile, Emilie stressed the importance of speaking good English and displaying impeccable English-style manners if he was to fit into the Canadian upper class. She encouraged him to speak English at every opportunity, discussed various aspects of the English mind with him, and worked on his table manners and dress. Eventually, her tutoring paid off. As the first Québécois prime minister, Wilfrid would be noted for his command of English and his ability to understand English sensibilities.

When Wilfrid was elected to Parliament and went

to Ottawa, he and Emilie wrote each other at least twice a week. After he became prime minister in June 1896, it was natural that he would find some means of bringing Emilie to the nation's capital. It took a year, but in the summer of 1897, he appointed Lavergne judge of the Superior Court in the District of Hull.

Almost immediately, Emilie became one of the most popular hostesses in the capital. Her flair for fashion, her understanding of politics, and her talents as a hostess made it easy to see why Wilfrid found her fascinating. Lacking Emilie's stylish panache, Zöe paled by comparison.

Accompanying the Lavergnes were their two children, Gabrielle and Armand. According to contemporary gossip, both children were Wilfrid's. The prime minister regarded Gabrielle with such affection that he paid for part of her schooling. On her 21st birthday, in the midst of a serious crisis over Canadian involvement in the Boer War, Wilfrid found time to write to her. And as Armand grew older, his resemblance to the prime minister inspired much gossip.

Lavergne ignored the gossip, preferring to live in peace. And the affection Wilfrid felt for the Lavergne children may have stemmed from his not having children of his own. Perhaps the most weighty argument against Laurier's paternity, however, is that Emilie ultimately lost her hold over him. At a vice-regal dinner in 1900, she argued loudly with a visiting Boer War hero, Winston Churchill. She also openly expressed pro-Boer sentiments.

Her outspokenness upset Laurier, who was trying hard to weather a serious political storm caused by the war. Shortly after Emilie's outburst, he returned all the letters she had written him. Soon afterwards, Joseph was transferred to Montreal, and Emilie had no choice but to accompany him.

Emilie and Wilfrid corresponded for a time, but gradually their relationship deteriorated into squabbles over money. In 1909, when Lavergne's expected appointment as Quebec chief justice failed to materialize, Emilie and Laurier were no longer in touch.

By this time, Zöe had taken a leaf from her rival's book. She had found a skilled seamstress and learned to dress with style. She had also learned to wield power in the nation's capital and to speak English competently. In the long run, the quiet fidelity of the unambitious Zöe outlasted the scintillating brilliance of her rival.

Chapter 6
Scandalous Affairs

From the time of Marc Antony to the era of Bill Clinton, sex has played an important role in politics. Sometimes, the consequences of a politician's sexual antics have been tragic, sometimes humorous — and sometimes a mixture of both. What's certain is that the sexual activities of public figures have always been a favourite target of gossip.

Walter Patterson, the first governor of Prince Edward Island, was one public figure who found his sexual activities subjected to careful scrutiny, with dire results for his political career. Born in County Donegal,

Ireland, in about 1735, Walter spent his early life in the British army, serving in both Ireland and North America. After retiring from military life in 1764, he became involved in colonial land speculation.

In 1769, he was appointed governor of the Island of St. John, known today as Prince Edward Island. At the time, the colony boasted a little more than 300 inhabitants, most of them French-speaking. Walter, the newly appointed council, and the supreme court were charged with the mission of establishing British institutions there.

This was easier said that done. Walter had trouble finding suitable men to fill offices and frequently found himself drawn into the land disputes that had split the government into various factions.

At first, Walter put up a brave front. "A few years Peace... will make this one of the most flourishing Governments in America," he wrote on July 6, 1780. A little more than two months later, he was writing a letter of introduction for a friend, John Stewart, to carry to England. "Mr. Stewart is a Friend of mine of long standing," he noted. But the friendship would soon fall apart, and Stewart would help ruin Walter's career.

In 1784, Walter dissolved the colony's assembly so that he could introduce an unpopular tax. Led by Stewart, the speaker of the house, assembly members objected. For Stewart, the objection was more than political. It was also very personal.

Stewart's father, Peter, was chief justice of the island. In the fall of 1782, he had been stricken by rheumatism. Walter visited frequently to cheer him up and often brought along remedies to help ease his friend's suffering. The governor's visits had more than one purpose, however, as Peter Stewart wrote some time later. "While I attributed his apparent anxiety to disinterested Friendship, was he using his utmost efforts to seduce my Wife, with whom I have always lived in the most cordial affection. At last, when my life was much despaired of he succeeded, of which there is the clearest proof possible."

Sarah Hamilton had married Peter Stewart in Scotland in 1770, after the death of his second wife, Helen. According to traditional accounts, Sarah was a devout Roman Catholic and an accomplished needlewoman. She was also interested in literature and wrote poetry to amuse herself and others.

As a dutiful wife, she had accompanied her husband and his children across the Atlantic. A navigational error brought their ship to the north shore of the island, rather than the south, and before the passengers were able to disembark, a sudden gale drove the ship onto the beach and wrecked it. The passengers and crew set up camp and, as the days grew steadily colder, waited for rescue that was several weeks in coming.

This was not an auspicious beginning for Sarah Stewart's life in her new home, and conditions soon went from bad to worse. In the makeshift colonial society of the island, her talents found few outlets, and sheer boredom may have persuaded her to succumb to the governor's advances.

In a community as small as the island, the liaison could hardly remain secret for long, especially as both Sarah and Walter were married. Peter Stewart's pride was wounded, and he threw his wife out of the house. He then started legal proceedings against the governor.

With no one else to turn to, Sarah went to Walter for help. There was no question of the governor's living openly with the discarded wife of the chief justice, especially with legal proceedings in the works. Peter Stewart reported what happened next.

> [Walter Patterson] *sent the unhappy Deluded Woman, and one of our sons from the Island. He not only conducted them from this place by day light on the 6th of August last, but carried the boy behind him on his own Horse to the north coast, where he had a schooner prepared for their reception, and ship'd them off for Canada, where they still remain.*

Meanwhile, believing that the best defence is a good offence, Walter mounted a counterattack against Peter Stewart. The governor's supporters did their best to discredit the chief justice, writing to the colonial office with a different version of events. Walter claimed that the report of his adulterous relationship with Sarah was "a vile, false story" made up by Peter Stewart's children from his earlier marriage "on purpose to get rid of a step-Mother." He tried to portray himself as a chivalrous gentleman, coming to the rescue of a damsel in distress.

The colonial office secretaries must have shaken their heads at the mess Walter had created for himself. And things were not about to get better. His position had been downgraded from governor to lieutenant-governor, and he now reported directly to the governor of Nova Scotia. Then came word that he had been removed from office.

On his return to England, Walter made several futile attempts to regain favour and his fortune. Eventually, he was thrown into debtors' prison, and upon his relief, lived in poverty until his death in September 1798.

As for Sarah, she was apparently never completely reconciled with her husband, although she did return to the island. Peter Stewart died in 1805 and was buried in the English Church Cemetery in Charlottetown. When

Sarah died 23 years later, at the age of 84, her body was laid to rest in St. Andrew's Roman Catholic cemetery, some distance from her husband's grave, and farther still from that of Walter Patterson, whose passion for her had helped destroy his career.

Although the behaviour of Walter Patterson and Sarah Stewart scandalized the society in which they lived, both Walter and Sarah's husband looked for a peaceful, legal way of settling their differences. John Wilson and Robert Lyon did not. On June 13, 1833, the two men raised their pistols and faced each other across a ploughed field on the bank of the River Tay. It was 6 P.M. and despite the heavy rain, the two law students had met to settle a point of honour. As their seconds watched, they took aim.

The duel would be the last in Upper Canada, and a woman was the cause of it.

Born in Scotland in about 1790, John had come to Canada as a child. While teaching school, he was noticed by a Perth lawyer, James Boulton. In exchange for tutoring one of Boulton's children, John was given accommodations and a chance to study law. Through his legal connections, he met Lyon, another law student who was five years younger.

Both men knew Elizabeth Hughes, who taught

school in Perth. With her father, a clergyman, and younger brother, Elizabeth had immigrated to Canada from England in 1832. Soon after their arrival, Reverend Hughes had died of cholera, and Elizabeth and her 12-year-old brother were taken in by family friends, the Acklands.

John courted Elizabeth for a time, but he gradually lost interest when he was attracted by another woman. Still, he found himself unable to tell Elizabeth about the changes in his feelings. Then, early in 1833, he and Lyon were in Bytown — now Ottawa — on business. Lyon made an insulting comment about Elizabeth, claiming that she was not a proper lady. John not only used the accusation to make the break with Elizabeth, but also reported the remarks to Mr. Ackland and other friends.

Eventually, the story was repeated to a young woman Lyon was courting — and she snubbed him for his ungentlemanly behaviour. Blaming John for the young woman's coldness, Lyon knocked him down the next time they met and called him a liar.

This was considered one of the worst insults possible. As a poor farmer's son who depended on Boulton's charity for advancement, John was keenly sensitive to the opinions of others. He believed that failing to respond to Lyon's insult would mean losing his hard-won social status. So at the urging of friends, John challenged

Lyon to a duel, not only to avenge the insult to him, but also in retaliation for the slur on Elizabeth's character.

Surprised by the challenge, Lyon claimed that his remarks about Elizabeth had been meant only to tease. Later, it was suggested he made them to please Henry Le Lievre, a relative who had been one of Elizabeth's suitors before John arrived on the scene. Lyon did not want to fight but finally succumbed to the pressure of his peers.

Though duels were illegal in both Upper and Lower Canada, they occurred frequently enough that a complex ritual had evolved. In most instances, the arrangements were made by seconds, who were supposed to do everything in their power to prevent bloodshed, either by encouraging the duellists to deliberately miss their targets or by persuading them to make peace before shots were fired. Lyon's second — Le Lievre, the man who may have started the trouble — was a particularly bad choice.

Although Lyon was reputedly a marksman, both he and John were off target when they fired their first shots. With honour satisfied, the two were willing to forget their differences, but Le Lievre insisted on a second exchange and refused to allow the attending physician to speak to Lyon.

Reluctantly, the duellists prepared for another round. Seconds later, Lyon lay on the damp ground, mortally wounded. He was carried to the home of his employer, Thomas Maybee Radenhurst, where he died. Meanwhile, Le Lievre fled, and John and his second, Simon Robertson, gave themselves up, fully aware that they would be charged with murder.

The trial took place on August 9. As accused felons, the young law students were denied counsel but ably defended themselves and won acquittal. After the trial, John and Elizabeth were reconciled and later married. Though he eventually established a prosperous law firm in London and entered politics, John spent the rest of his life regretting Lyon's premature death.

John may have unconsciously blamed his wife for the tragedy, for Elizabeth had her own bitter memories to deal with. She lived until 1904, never able to forget the insult Lyon had levelled against her. As an old woman, she was unable to sit comfortably in a Toronto streetcar in the presence of Lyon's relatives, and, it was said, she despised all members of the Lyon family until the end of her life.

Through much of Canadian history, a woman's value has been determined by her sexual behaviour. Young women were supposed to remain chaste until marriage. Laws were designed to protect them from seducers, and, if they did suffer what some people described as "a fate worse than death," penalties could be imposed. These often involved jail terms for the seducer and financial compensation for the woman's father, on the grounds that his daughter's loss of virginity diminished her value in the marriage market.

Attitudes had changed considerably by the 1930s. Nevertheless, one of the most notorious political scandals of the decade came to light in an Edmonton courtroom in 1934. John Edward Brownlee, premier of Alberta since 1925, was charged with the seduction of Vivian MacMillan, an unemployed typist.

John Brownlee was one of the most capable premiers the province had ever elected. Largely at his insistence, the province regained control of its natural resources. But as the Depression deepened, so did dissatisfaction with Brownlee's government. Because economic conditions had deteriorated during his term in office, many people held him responsible.

For many Albertans, Brownlee symbolized the enemy, the rich, sleek, fat cats who prospered while workers sank deeper and deeper into poverty and despair. It didn't help that he was an Easterner. Son of a small-town merchant in Port Ryerse, Ontario, Brownlee moved to Alberta in 1909, at the age of 26. Pursuing a legal career, he became solicitor for the United Farmers of Alberta, and when the party won the provincial election in 1921, he was appointed attorney general.

The slick, well-educated, prosperous lawyer-politician from the decadent East was accused of seducing an innocent small town girl, whom he had lured to the city with the promise of a job. In July 1930, Brownlee visited the small town of Edson, west of Edmonton, where Mayor Allan D. MacMillan introduced the premier to his 18-year-old daughter. Tall, slim, and delicately pretty, Vivian was an active member of the local Baptist Church, where she played the organ and taught Sunday school. Vivian claimed Brownlee complimented her on her beauty and suggested that if she came to Edmonton to enrol in a business course, he would act as her guardian and find her a government job.

That fall, Vivian moved to the provincial capital. Soon after her arrival, Brownlee invited her to his home. She visited the premier, his wife, and children several times. As Brownlee drove Vivian home after one visit, he arranged to meet her on his own. It was the first of several clandestine meetings.

According to Vivian, the premier told her that he was lonely and desperately needed someone to understand him. For years, he told her, he and his wife had slept apart because she was an invalid who would probably not survive another pregnancy. If Vivian did not give in to him, he would have to turn to his wife. She

Vivian MacMillan

would become pregnant, his family would be ruined, and he would not be able to go on as premier.

Vivian hesitated, telling Brownlee that because she cared for both him and his wife, she would do anything to help them. But wasn't there some other way?

There was not, Brownlee assured her. He kissed her, drove her home, and asked her to think about what he had said.

The next night, they met again, and Brownlee drove to a secluded spot outside the city. Persuading

John Brownlee

Vivian to move to the back seat with him, he repeated his request, then tried to force himself on her. When she resisted, Brownlee became furious and drove her back to town.

A few nights later, Vivian agreed to another meeting. This time, although she tried to fight him off, Brownlee had his way. According to Vivian's testimony, they met two or three times a week for the next three years.

Twice during their relationship, Vivian was an overnight guest in the Brownlee home. Both times, she and the premier met in secret, despite the risk of being heard by Brownlee's wife, his son Jack, or the maid. In court, Vivian described the elaborate precautions they took to escape detection. At night, Brownlee went to the bathroom and ran the water. Camouflaged by the noise, Vivian got out of bed and waited by the maid's door. Then Brownlee took her by the hand, and they timed their steps carefully so it sounded as if only one person were walking through the house. In the room he shared with his son, Brownlee stood between the beds while Vivian slipped beneath the covers. At other times, she said, they met in the legislative buildings.

On several occasions, Vivian testified, she had tried to end the relationship. When she pleaded for freedom, Brownlee became angry. Once, she said, he drove her home and pushed her out of the car rather than discuss a final break. He also sneered at the job she had found in the attorney general's office after finishing her business course, telling her that she had got it only through his influence. If she refused him, he warned, she might as well forget about the job.

Vivian began to lose weight and, in the spring of 1932, was hospitalized with what was described as a "nervous ailment." But she was unable to stop meeting Brownlee. "I seemed to be under his spell ... I couldn't stop going out with him; his influence was too strong."

The crisis came in 1933, when Vivian fell in love with John Caldwell, a medical student. When Caldwell proposed marriage, Vivian told him everything. Although Caldwell commiserated with her, he withdrew his offer.

Shortly afterwards, Vivian lost her job. She went home to Edson and confessed everything to her family. Then Vivian and her father launched a lawsuit, seeking $10,000 in damages from the premier.

Vivian's testimony made headlines across the country. Then defence witnesses took the stand, and discrepancies in her story began to emerge. Defence lawyer A.L. Smith showed that she was confused about one of the cars that had been used in her outings with Brownlee. On some of the dates she claimed they had been together, Brownlee had been out of town. When janitors from the legislative building were called to the stand, none recalled seeing Vivian anywhere near the premier's offices. Other testimony revealed that Brownlee had never approached the attorney general's office to request special treatment for Vivian.

The most credible witness of all may have been Florence Brownlee. The premier's wife refused to believe that her husband had committed adultery. She recalled their fondness of Vivian, how they had treated her like a daughter. Further evidence revealed that Florence was a light sleeper who could not possibly have slumbered through all the activity that was purportedly taking place at night. Moreover, she was not the invalid Vivian said Brownlee had described. True, doctors had diagnosed incipient tuberculosis several years earlier, but she was fully recovered. In fact, Florence played golf, rode horses, and canoed whenever the opportunity arose.

The jury of six — the usual number for a civil suit — refused to be swayed by the discrepancies in Vivian's testimony. The image of the innocent, vulnerable young woman was strong in their minds, especially after the Brownlees' attractive maid took the stand. Jessie Elgert swore she saw Brownlee take Vivian for a drive one night and hinted that this hardly surprised her, as she had gone out with the premier herself. Elgert's testimony created the impression that Brownlee habitually seduced beautiful young women.

Brownlee's own actions also damaged his case. When the suit was launched, the premier charged that Vivian and Caldwell had tried to extort money from him in exchange for their silence. Later, he withdrew the charges, saying that neither had ever asked for money.

The trial lasted a week. As the jury retired to consider its verdict, Justice William Ives warned that much of the evidence was based on Vivian's version of events. In essence, the jurors had to choose between Vivian's word and that of the premier.

The jury found Brownlee guilty of seduction and awarded $10,000 to Vivian and $5,000 to her father. Brownlee submitted his resignation immediately. But while the Alberta caucus deliberated over a successor, Justice Ives overruled the jury's decision to award damages to the MacMillans. Although this did not change the guilty verdict, the judge's ruling meant that no compensation would be paid.

Vivian and her father appealed the decision, but the ruling stood, as it was based on legal precedents that rarely compensated victims of seduction unless they were pregnant. Supported by the *Edmonton Bulletin*, whose reporters had been jailed for contempt by Justice Ives, Vivian took the case to the Supreme Court of Canada. On March 1, 1937, more than six years after the first furtive encounter with Brownlee, the court ruled in Vivian's favour.

Brownlee launched an appeal of his own, taking the case to the court of last resort, the Judicial Committee of the Privy Council in London, England. He lost and was ordered to pay damages. Brownlee learned, as so many politicians have before and since, that those in public office are more vulnerable than most to the hint of sexual scandal.

Chapter 7
Grow Old with Me

The grand passions of young lovers are often too hot to survive for long. In contrast, the deep and abiding affection of couples who live together for many years, through laughter and sorrow, sickness and health, often proves to be the sweetest love of all.

Such was the case for James and Amelia Douglas. In 1828, while his father-in-law and boss, William Connolly, was away, James was placed in charge of Fort St. James, a Hudson's Bay Company trading post in New Caledonia, which would later become British Columbia. Connolly's decision to leave the young man at the helm nearly ended in disaster.

Some time earlier, two traders had been killed by members of the Carrier nation. James was determined to punish the murderers, and according to one account, went right into the Carrier encampment and shot one of the killers point blank. Soon afterwards, a raiding party led by Chief Kwah attacked the fort, bent on killing James. The young man fought off the attackers, kicking and swearing until he was exhausted. Then he tried to reason with them. They refused to listen, and two men held knives to his throat, begging the chief's permission to kill him.

Meanwhile, Amelia, James's bride, and Nancy Boucher, wife of the fort interpreter, gathered blankets, tobacco, and cloth from the storeroom and flung the goods on the ground in front of the invaders, bargaining for James's life. Eventually, Kwah and his men accepted the trade and departed peacefully.

This was not the first time his temper had plunged James into trouble. Born in 1803 in Demerara, British Guiana (now Guyana), James was the son of a wealthy Scottish merchant involved in raising sugar cane. The merchant had never married, but his liaison with a black woman produced three children, James, William and Cecilia. As a child, James was sent to school in Scotland, and according to family tradition, he also spent time in England, where he learned French from an émigré. At the age of 16, he entered the fur trade with the North West Company. He joined the Hudson's Bay Company when it took over the Nor'Westers.

A studious young man who brought a library of 45 books with him to Western Canada, Douglas worked as a clerk and trader and was soon recognized as a "promising young man" who could expect regular promotions.

His major fault was his violent temper, which once resulted in a duel with another Hudson's Bay employee. Fortunately, no blood was shed, but Connolly took the young man aside and warned him to keep his temper in check, especially where Aboriginal people were concerned. The traders needed their friendship, not only to ensure continued profits from the fur trade, but also to survive in the hostile wilderness. Anxious to improve himself in any way possible, James took Connolly's words to heart and made an effort to control his anger.

He succeeded well enough for Connolly to accept him as a husband for his daughter, Amelia. One of Connolly's children with a Cree woman named Suzanne, Amelia was born at Norway House in what later became Manitoba. Sixteen at the time of her marriage, she was a gentle, shy, and retiring young woman with kind grey eyes and a complexion so fair that the men of Fort St. James called her Little Snowbird. Because there were few clergymen in New Caledonia, she and James were married "according to the custom of the country," just as Amelia's parents and several other fur traders at the fort had been.

In 1830, James was transferred to Fort Vancouver, in what is now the state of Washington. Built five years earlier, the fort was the capital of west coast fur trading and was much more "civilized" than New Caledonia. James left for his new post in January, while his wife stayed behind to care for their first child, who had been born in 1829. Before Amelia was able to join her husband in the spring, the baby died. Amelia subsequently gave birth to 12 more children, although only six reached adulthood.

Life at Fort Vancouver was easier than at Fort St. James. Offices and warehouses, workshops, a schoolhouse, and a chapel made it more like a small town than a remote trading outpost. Nearby farms provided a variety of food, and a steady stream of visitors kept the fort's inhabitants in contact with the outside world. Typically, visitors were entertained in the mess hall where the men dined. The women, all of whom had Aboriginal blood, were restricted to their own quarters, a situation that the timid Amelia found completely acceptable.

Dr. John McLoughlin, chief factor of the Hudson's Bay Company's Columbia Department, admired James and helped foster his career. Soon after his arrival at Fort

Vancouver, James was named chief trader, at the handsome salary of £400 a year.

While James's career flourished and Amelia cared for their children, civilization was encroaching on the fort. One of the first signs that times were changing was the arrival in 1836 of the company chaplain, Rev. Herbert Beaver, and his wife, a woman of stiff principles. Mrs. Beaver snubbed the half-Aboriginal wives at the fort because none had been married in a church ceremony.

As the wife of an important official, Amelia might have been insulted, although her shyness and hesitant English would have prevented much conversation with the minister's wife. James, on the other hand, was angered by Mrs. Beaver's treatment of Amelia. To set matters right, he remarried his wife in a ceremony officiated by Rev. Beaver on February 28, 1837.

This was unusual at the time. Fur traders typically lived in common-law arrangements with Aboriginal women, sometimes for decades. These relationships were based not only on physical attraction, but also on mutual economic benefit. Through their "country wives," the traders forged connections with the people who supplied furs. The Aboriginal women provided a knowledge of local language and customs and an array of domestic services, such as making moccasins, that helped their men survive. In exchange, the women and their children enjoyed a measure of status and economic security. Sons often followed theirs fathers into the fur trade, while daughters married traders.

But there was also a nasty side to the arrangement. At the end of their careers, many men in the fur trade abandoned their Aboriginal wives and children when they returned to "civilization" in Eastern Canada or Britain.

Amelia's own father had seemed to be an exception. In 1831, he had taken her mother and younger siblings with him to Eastern Canada. But the next year, he left his family to marry a white woman. James's decision to marry Amelia in a church ceremony made it clear that he had no intention of following his father-in-law's example.

By 1840, James was chief factor, the highest position in the company's field operations. His duties often involved international politics and diplomacy — and he was appointed governor of Vancouver Island in 1851. Within a decade, he was governor of British Columbia.

As the top official in the new colony, James insisted on all the ceremony that was due him. Meanwhile, Amelia stayed out of the limelight. For one thing, she was more comfortable speaking French and Cree than English. For another, as more and more white women reached the Northwest, the women of mixed blood who had made early settlement possible were increasingly treated as inferior. Rather than face even subtle prejudice, Amelia refused to attend official functions, although she did host regular picnics for area children When she was not involved in caring for her own family or household duties, she looked after her chickens and gardens. All the same, on the rare occasions when she was persuaded to receive visitors, she was always a kind and considerate hostess.

When James retired in 1864, he was knighted, and for once, Amelia overcame her shyness to participate in the ceremony. In March, 1864, she accompanied her husband to New Westminster to await the arrival of the new governor While there, the couple attended a ceremonial dinner, and the four elected representatives of the legislative council presented Amelia with a plaster medallion bearing a likeness of her husband.

James and Amelia lived contently together until his death of a heart attack in August 1874. By the time Amelia died in 1890, British Columbia had been transformed into a world far removed from the trading post where two racially mixed young people had fallen in love.

As James and Amelia Douglas were enjoying the first years of his retirement, the events that would bring together another couple were just starting to unfold.

Grow Old with Me

When Louis Riel emerged as the leader of the Red River Resistance in 1869, he started down a path that led to the destruction of his family and the end of his own life. Paradoxically, the same events that separated Marguerite and Louis Riel brought two other lovers together. Unlike the Riels, who were seldom apart for more than a few days until Louis's arrest and imprisonment, James Macleod and Mary Drever were forced apart so many times and for such long periods that it sometimes seemed as if the fates were conspiring against them.

James was born on the Scottish Isle of Skye on September 25, 1836, and immigrated to Canada with his family in 1845. Although his parents planned a professional career for him, he was happiest trekking through the woods near the family home in Richmond Hill, north of Toronto. He often encountered Ojibwa during these hikes and gained a deep appreciation of their ways. He also learned their language, tracking and hunting skills, how to walk on snowshoes, and how to survive in the woods on the coldest nights.

By the time James graduated from Upper Canada College, he was a lean and attractive young man, just under six feet tall, with golden hair and an erect, graceful bearing. He was also something of a hellraiser, preferring wine and women to his studies. As a result, he twice failed the law school entrance examinations. His father was furious, though not nearly as angry as he became in 1856, when he learned that James had joined the Kingston Voluntary Field Battery as a lieutenant. By 1867, having served in the Fenian raids with distinction, James had achieved the rank of major.

Although he finally set up a law practice in Bowmanville, James was hungry for adventure. In 1870, when the Red River Rebellion erupted in what is now Manitoba, he was among the soldiers sent west under General Garnet Wolseley.

Meanwhile, Mary was playing her own role in the rebellion. The daughter of William Drever, a retired Hudson's Bay Company employee, Mary was born in October 1852 in the Red River Colony. With her sisters and brother Willie, Mary grew up in a close-knit community that included a number of Métis families. The family cottage was full of books, so the Drever children were well educated by community standards. But not all their learning came from books. Willie rode, hunted, and tracked as well as any of the Métis, and Mary was not far behind him when it came to riding a horse.

As the railway moved westward and the Métis found their way of life threatened, they rebelled. Though there was considerable sympathy for them in some parts of the community, there were also deep divisions. At one point, Willie was arrested for opposing Riel's actions. Knowing Riel would not use force when a woman was involved, Mary's father sent her to plead for her brother's release. A few days later, Willie and some of the other prisoners were freed, just in time to celebrate the New Year. On January 2, Mary and some friends baked files into cakes and delivered them to the remaining prisoners. A short time later, several of the captives escaped.

Furious at this treachery, Riel demanded that the Drevers surrender to his government. When they refused, he ordered his men to aim a cannon at Rothney Cottage, the family's home, and told them to come out. Mary stood at the window while her father calmly ate his breakfast in full view of Riel's men. Eventually, the rebel leader withdrew the cannons, although he took William Drever into custody and confiscated all the horses except a lame mare. Later, Mary rode this mare to take a message to General Wolseley's troops, who were then about 50 kilometres from the settlement.

By the time Wolseley and his soldiers marched into the settlement, Riel and his men had withdrawn. But the arrival of government troops was cause for celebration. At Rothney Cottage, the Drevers served rum to all visitors. Brigade Major James Macleod was among their guests.

Before long, James was a regular caller at the

cottage. He and Mary chatted, walked, and rode together on the prairie. Soon, he was escorting her to entertainments in the community. In early 1871, James proposed. Mary accepted and ordered her wedding dress from Scotland, where her parents had been born.

Before the wedding date could be set, however, James learned that he was being ordered back to Toronto. Mary refused to go. Her mother had died in 1867, her older sisters were married, and she would not abandon her ailing father. When no amount of persuasion could change her mind, the couple broke their engagement, and James returned to Ontario, where he was honoured as a hero.

Meanwhile, more trouble was brewing, this time in the Saskatchewan district. With his experience and reputation, James felt sure that he could persuade authorities to send him there. This would bring him close to Mary again. As he waited, he visited his widowed mother, describing Mary in loving detail. Still no word came. By 1872, he had more or less given up hope of returning to the prairies.

Then, in Fort Garry, the commanding officer resigned. Because James had been second in command for a time, he seemed a natural choice to replace Colonel William Osborne-Smith. James wrote to his friend Alexander Campbell, a former law partner of

Prime Minister John A. Macdonald, asking for his help. When no reply came, he left for England, where he hoped to find work.

In Winnipeg, Mary heard the news and told her friends that if James failed to return, she would marry anyone just to be near him in England. Her friends teased, but she was adamant, remembering the Scottish wedding dress packed away in its cedar box.

James was visiting relatives in Scotland when the prime minister offered him a commission as a superintendent in the newly formed North-West Mounted Police. As soon as he could, James returned to Canada.

James was third in command of the contingent of 150 Mounties who rode into Fort Garry that fall. Dressed in scarlet tunics, blue breeches, and white helmets with plumes, the men were an impressive sight — and none more so that Superintendent Macleod. Among the crowd waiting to greet the Mounties was Mary.

When they finally came face to face, James burst out laughing as Mary coquettishly batted her eyelashes behind a fan. She wanted to make it clear that she was a match for any of the sophisticated ladies he had met in Eastern Canada and Britain. As far as James was concerned, however, no one came close to matching Mary. They were engaged immediately and set the wedding date for the following July.

James Macleod

In the spring, Mary and her sisters started sewing and baking for the wedding, which was to be one of the most important social events of the season. The plans went awry, though, when James was promoted to assistant commissioner and ordered west to present-day Alberta. Able to offer Mary no home but a tent and unwilling to risk making her a widow early in their marriage, James postponed the wedding.

The next 18 months were hell for James and his

Mary Drever Macleod

men. From their headquarters, named Fort Macleod in James's honour, they patrolled 800,000 square kilometres of prairie in search of bootleg whiskey and lawless traders. They won the confidence of Chief Crowfoot's Blackfoot nation and battled heat, insects, and freezing weather. Through it all, James managed to keep up morale, although they had little contact with the outside world. Worse, no payroll arrived until the spring of 1875.

By the end of that year, James had decided to resign

from the force to become a stipendiary magistrate for the district. He was shocked by Ottawa 's neglect and had little respect for Commissioner Arthur French, the NWMP's commanding officer.

Then French left the force, and James agreed to replace him. His duties were to begin on July 20, 1876. Early in June, he arrived in Winnipeg. His brothers met him, bringing a wedding ring their mother had chosen for Mary. Once more, preparations for a magnificent wedding were started. And once again, James was called away. On June 24, Sitting Bull led the Sioux against American general George Custer at Little Big Horn, then fled to safety in Canada.

While NWMP Inspector James Walsh almost single-handedly persuaded the Sioux to lay down their weapons, James rushed to Ottawa to advise the Canadian government of the situation. As soon as his official duty was done, he travelled by train through the United States, reaching Winnipeg on July 28. Forewarned of his schedule, Mary was fastening her wedding gown when he arrived at Rothney Cottage. The elaborate wedding they had planned was forgotten. At five o'clock that evening, before most of the town realized James was back, the two were married in a quiet ceremony. The next day, James rode off to join his men, and Mary went east to visit his mother.

Duty kept the newlyweds apart until 1877, when James asked Mary to meet him in Chicago. For what must have seemed like hours, she waited in the cold, then, discouraged, found a cab to take her back to her hotel. As it pulled out of the station, she heard someone call her name and looked out to see James leaning out the window of another cab, waving and calling to her. As the two cabs slid to a stop, Mary and James rushed onto the icy street and into each other's arms, ignoring the startled passers-by.

They quarrelled almost immediately. The first council of the North-West Territories was about to meet, and James's presence was required. When Mary protested, he gave her three choices: stay alone in Chicago, return to his mother's home, or go with him. Mary chose to go with him.

After visiting her family in Winnipeg, they made a honeymoon trip by dogsled to Swan River, then travelled east to Ottawa, where they were entertained by the governor general. Eventually, James brought his bride to Fort Macleod. He was the first Mountie to do this, and both his men and the officials in Ottawa worried that Mary's presence would cause trouble. Instead, she brought a touch of civilization to the isolated outpost. Within a few years, other Mounties' wives joined her.

Mary accompanied James whenever she could and

was one of six white women to sign historic Treaty Number 7 with the Blackfoot nation. Too often, though, the two were separated, first by James's duties, then by Mary's frequent visits to the East, especially after their children were sent to school there. Whenever they were apart, they wrote letters. At Mary's insistence, James burned all hers, but his attest to the happiness of their marriage. In 1890, when she sent a photograph of herself, James was delighted. "I never saw a more perfect picture of a perfect woman," he wrote.

By this time, they were living in Calgary at least part of the time. Both James and Mary were pained by their frequent separations, but neither considered putting personal feelings first. Even as James's health failed in the spring and summer of 1894, he carried out his duties, although the sight of Mary waving goodbye with a handkerchief pressed to her eyes hurt him as much as the prospect of being away from her.

The final separation came September 5, when James died in Mary's arms. After an elaborate funeral, complete with an NWMP escort, Mary learned that James had left little money and many debts. She moved in with her sister's family. When the government refused to provide a pension for James's dedicated service, local residents raised enough to send his son to school and buy a house for his family.

Mary supported herself by sewing fashionable dresses for society ladies. In 1927, she was one of the guests of honour at a Calgary banquet celebrating the 50th anniversary of the Blackfoot treaty. The woman who had defied Louis Riel wept when she was made an honorary member of the NWMP Veterans' Association and presented with a bouquet of roses. After the ceremony, there were more tears when she placed the flowers on James's grave, plucking one blossom from the bouquet as a keepsake.

Although she was only 42 when James died, Mary never remarried. In quiet times, she sat in what had been James's favourite chair, reading and re-reading his letters. One of the last was especially poignant. In it, James described how he was sending her some wild roses he had found. He was so lonely, he wrote. "Darling … I do so long to see you, and may Heaven grant we may never be separated so long again. With endless love … Jim."

Duty kept Mary and James Macleod apart during much of their married life, and death separated them far too soon. But another couple was far more fortunate.

In the fall of 1871, 15-year-old Mabel Hubbard climbed Boston's Beacon Hill with Mary True, her former teacher. Daughter of a prominent lawyer, Gardiner Greene Hubbard, Mabel had been left completely deaf at the age of five by a bout of scarlet fever. Thanks to the efforts of her parents and the devotion of Miss True, she had learned to lip read so well that new acquaintances had difficulty believing she was deaf. The only hint of her condition was a certain tonelessness in her speech. This often made it difficult for strangers to understand her.

Now Mabel was on her way to lessons that might help improve her speech. Her professor was to be Alexander Graham Bell, a relative newcomer to Boston. As they walked, Miss True praised Professor Bell and his methods so highly that Mabel decided that he must be a fraud. Her opinion was reinforced when they reached his rooms.

Because of her deafness, Mabel could not hear Bell's wonderful voice and the Scottish accent that had charmed many others. Instead, she had to base her initial opinion on what she saw — and she was not impressed. Tall and thin, Professor Bell was carelessly dressed in a dark, old-fashioned suit. Mabel decided that she did not like him.

Alexander Graham Bell, or Aleck, as he was called by his family, was born on March 3, 1847, in Edinburgh, Scotland. His father, Alexander Melville Bell, was a prominent teacher and elocutionist who was particularly interested in work with the deaf and had, in fact, married a deaf woman. It seemed as if Aleck and his two older brothers would follow in their father's footsteps. But when Ted and Melville succumbed to tuberculosis, the elder Bell decided to emigrate to Canada, where the air was cleaner and his youngest son had a better chance for survival.

The family settled at Tutela Heights, near Brantford, Ontario. Aleck spent his first Canadian summer relaxing with books and blankets on the bluffs above the Grand River, but by autumn, he was anxious for independence. His chance came when he was offered a job at a school for the deaf in Boston. Although the opportunity vanished when the school ran into financial problems, he had made enough connections to set himself up as a tutor for deaf students. Before long, he was giving lessons to about 20 people.

In some cases, his relationship with the students and their families was purely professional. But Hubbard was very interested in education for the deaf and invited Aleck to his home from time to time. During one of those visits, Aleck talked of scientific theories that would eventually lead to the invention of the telephone. Hubbard, a patent lawyer, was immediately interested and provided useful contacts and encouragement.

In the meantime, Aleck had fallen in love with Mabel.

For a time, he refused to acknowledge his feelings.

He was in no position to support a wife, especially one who was the daughter of a socially prominent lawyer and would naturally expect to lead a similar lifestyle after her marriage. So Aleck tried to draw satisfaction from his role as Mabel's teacher and family friend. Then he learned that Mabel was going Nantucket for the summer. Faced with the prospect of separation, he revealed his feelings in a letter to her mother, Gertrude. And because he realized that the Hubbards might not welcome his attentions to their daughter, he promised to abide by any decision they made.

Fortunately, the Hubbards were fond of their daughter's tutor. They asked only that he wait a year before declaring his feelings to Mabel. By that time, she would be older and more sure of her own mind.

Aleck agreed to the Hubbards' conditions and focused on his work. Soon afterwards, the telephone proved its feasibility when Thomas Watson heard Aleck's voice for the first time. Though he was elated by the breakthrough, Aleck found himself brooding about Mabel and regretting his promise to her parents.

Meanwhile, Mabel learned of Aleck's feelings from her older cousin, Mary Blatchford, with whom she was staying in Nantucket. Mary disliked like Aleck, though she would later grow quite fond of him, and undoubtedly emphasized all his bad points as she talked to her young cousin. Upset and confused, Mabel wrote to her mother, asking for advice. In the letter, she said that no matter how intelligent Mr. Bell might be, she could never love him, or for that matter, even like him completely.

When Gertrude read this letter to Aleck, he became terribly upset. Because Mabel now knew of his feelings, he reasoned, he owed her the respect of discussing them with her personally. He raced off to Nantucket.

Mabel refused to see him, so he poured out his heart in a letter. "Tell me frankly all that there is in me that you dislike that I can alter ... I wish to amend my life for you." He followed up with a note saying he would not bother her until the year her parents' had asked for was up.

Still, on her return to Boston, Mabel agreed to see him. As his hopes for winning Mabel's love grew, Aleck wrote defiantly to Gertrude. He said that as soon as he knew Mabel loved him, he wanted them to become engaged, and as soon as he could provide for her, he would marry her, whether this was in two months or two years. Gertrude, already fond of the passionate and stubborn young man, released him from his promise, telling him that if he could win Mabel's affection, she would be completely satisfied.

The courtship continued quietly until November 25, 1875, when Mabel celebrated her 18th birthday. It was also Thanksgiving, a holiday both Mabel and Aleck would cherish for the rest of their lives. When Aleck came to call that day, Mabel told him that she loved him better than anyone except her mother. They were engaged immediately.

Almost at once, Mabel began to wield her influence. She asked her fiancé to change the spelling of his name from Aleck to Alec, which she preferred. Alec readily agreed. Mabel was less successful, however, in her attempt to change his work habits. For a long time, he worked on his inventions at night, even if this made it hard to get up in the morning. Mabel was convinced that his nocturnal habits weren't quite respectable and asked him to change. He tried, without success. Exasperated, Mabel told him she was painting his portrait, then presented him with the picture of an owl.

In 1876, at Mabel's insistence, Alec demonstrated the telephone at a Philadelphia exposition celebrating the American centennial. Soon, the invention was attracting serious attention, and its inventor was earning money from lectures and demonstrations. Feeling that he could now support a wife, Alec discussed a wedding date with Mabel.

When income from the lectures dropped off, however, Alec became worried. At that point, Cupid stepped in, disguised as William H. Reynolds, who purchased a part-interest in the English patent on the telephone for $5,000 cash. The tidy nest egg paved the way for a wedding on July 11, 1877.

Aleck and Mabel were married in the Hubbard house. As wedding gifts, Alec gave Mabel a cross studded with pearls and most of his shares in the Bell Telephone Company, a total of about 30 percent of the stock. As Alec's invention grew in popularity, Mabel became independently wealthy.

With their money worries gone, the couple enjoyed a prolonged honeymoon in Canada and Britain. Six months after the marriage, Mabel wrote about Alec: "He is just as lovely as ever he can be, and instead of finding more faults in him, as they say married people always find in each other, I only find more to love and admire." This statement summed up the rest of their life together.

Alec and Mabel enjoyed a long, satisfying marriage because their personalities were complementary. Raised to be a society wife, Mabel was at ease in most situations. Alec, by contrast, was reserved except when alone with his family, and as he grew older, this tendency increased. Although he had a flair for drama and could confidently put his point across, he was not gregarious. As he confided to Mabel in 1883, he had many acquaintances, but few friends.

In effect, Mabel was his best friend. Just as she

fought her deafness in an effort to function normally, she helped her husband fight his solitary tendencies. Once, when Alec hid in the attic rather than face a social engagement, she tracked him down by the smell of his cigar. Without consciously considering it, she knew just how important social contacts were to his career.

And it wasn't just a matter of forcing Alec into a round of parties, receptions, and teas. Mabel was proud of her husband, especially as she realized how respected he was, and how impressive. She considered him the most distinguished-looking man in Washington — although not the most handsome, she teased.

For his part, Alec understood Mabel's efforts on his behalf, no matter how often he might try to hide from her. He also recognized her need for social contacts and entertainment. A common and very touching sight at the theatre in Washington, D.C., was big, bearded Alec Bell sitting with his head half turned toward his diminutive wife as he silently mouthed the dialogue so that she could follow the play by reading his lips.

Though the couple remained deeply in love, they also had their differences. They quarrelled about money, as Alec frequently ignored the household budget and gave money to nearly anyone who asked. Mabel solved this problem by taking over the household finances. She was less successful, however, in persuading her husband to give up his night-owl work habits.

Still, the differences between Alec and Mabel were surmountable in a life that was generally comfortable and happy. Tragedy also helped bring them closer. Two sons died of respiratory problems shortly after birth. Consoled by their surviving children, the Bells learned to live with their loss and eventually found great satisfaction in their grandchildren. Nowhere were they happier than at their summer retreat in Cape Breton, Nova Scotia.

Alec had never been able to tolerate the heat and humidity of Washington summers, and in 1885, he travelled with his father and Mabel to Canada's east coast on vacation. In Cape Breton, they stopped at Baddeck and immediately fell in love with the place. Together, Alec and Mabel built a summer home there and called it Beinn Bhreagh after a nearby peak. The words mean "beautiful mountain" in Gaelic.

Beinn Bhreagh was Alec and Mabel's haven, a place where they could walk hand in hand for hours, enjoying the scenery and quiet surroundings. It was only fitting that they should spend their last days together in their beloved summer home.

As he grew older, Alec had developed diabetes. For a while, he held his own, but in the summer of 1922, his health began to deteriorate. By July 31, he was only semi-conscious, but on August 1, he was lucid enough to carry on a conversation. Sometime during that day, he spoke of the happy life he had shared with Mabel.

His daughters and their husbands were nearby, and with Mabel, they kept vigil by his bed on the sleeping porch. That afternoon, Alec slipped into a half-conscious state, still holding Mabel's hand. As the sky darkened and the moon rose, Mabel removed her hand from her husband's and went to rest on a nearby sofa.

At about 2 A.M. on August 2, one of her sons-in-law called her. Mabel hurried to Alec's bedside and grasped his hand. "Alec," she whispered, and he opened his eyes, smiling, "don't leave me."

He clasped her hand, signing "no," then slipped away.

Alec had never liked mourning, and Mabel was certain that if she started wearing black, she would never return to brighter colors. At the funeral, she and her daughters wore white summer dresses. After a simple ceremony, Alec was buried atop Beinn Bhreagh.

Mabel was desolate. For most of her life, Alec had been the most important person in her world. As late as 1917, after 40 years of marriage, she had written: "It actually was almost as much as I could do to keep from crying when the train moved out and I couldn't see your white head any more."

Now, with Alec gone forever, there was nothing to stop her tears. She died five months later, on January 3, 1923, and was buried beside her husband.

Bibliography

Bruce, Robert V. *Bell: Alexander Graham Bell and the Conquest of Solitude.* Boston: Little, Brown, 1973.

Gillen, Molly. *The Prince and His Lady.* Toronto: Griffin House, 1970.

Gwyn, Sandra. *The Private Capital.* Toronto: McClelland and Stewart, 1984.

Smith, Donald B. *Sacred Feathers: The Reverend Peter Jones (Kahkewaquonaby) and the Mississauga Indians.* Toronto: University of Toronto Press, 1987.

Photo Credits

Cover: Whyte Museum of the Canadian Rockies; **Glenbow Archives:** pages 126 & 127; **National Archives of Canada:** pages 84 & 85; **Provincial Archives of Alberta:** pages 108 & 109.

Acknowledgments

The author acknowledges the assistance and encouragement of the following organizations and individuals: Acadia University, Special Collections; British Columbia Public Archives; Cambridge (Ontario) Public Library; John Robert Colombo; Glenbow Museum; Haldimand County Libraries (Selkirk Branch); Hamilton Public Library Special Collections; Library of Congress, Washington, D.C.; Kitchener Public Library; Manitoba Provincial Archives; McMaster University; National Archives of Canada; National Geographic Society; Tourism, Recreation and Heritage New Brunswick; Memorial University of Newfoundland; Newfoundland Historical Society; Provincial Archives of Newfoundland and Labrador; Department of Culture, Recreation and Fitness, Nova Scotia; Prince Edward Island Public Archives; Archives nationales du Québec; Saskatchewan Archives Board, Saskatoon and Regina; University Hospital, London, Ontario; Regional Collection, University of Western Ontario.

OTHER AMAZING STORIES

ISBN	Title	Author
1-55153-962-3	British Columbia Murders	Susan McNicoll
1-55153-966-7	Canadian Spies in WWII	Tom Douglas
1-55153-982-9	Dinosaur Hunters	Lisa Murphy-Lamb
1-55153-970-5	Early Voyageurs	Marie Savage
1-55153-996-9	Emily Carr	Cat Klerks
1-55153-968-3	Edwin Alonzo Boyd	Nate Hendley
1-55153-961-6	Étienne Brûlé	Gail Douglas
1-55153-993-4	Ghost Town Stories from the Canadian Rockies	Johnnie Bachusky
1-55153-992-6	Ghost Town Stories II from the Red Coat Trail	Johnnie Bachusky
1-55153-946-2	Great Dog Stories	Roxanne Snopek
1-55153-958-6	Hudson's Bay Company Adventures	Elle Andra-Warner
1-55153-969-1	Klondike Joe Boyle	Stan Sauerwein
1-55153-964-0	Marilyn Bell	Patrick Tivy
1-55153-962-4	Niagara Daredevils	Cheryl MacDonald
1-55153-981-0	Rattenbury	Stan Sauerwein
1-55153-991-8	Rebel Women	Linda Kupecek
1-55153-995-0	Rescue Dogs	Dale Portman
1-55153-997-7	Sam Steele	Holly Quan
1-55153-954-3	Snowmobile Adventures	Linda Aksomitis
1-55153-986-1	Tales from the West Coast	Adrienne Mason
1-55153-950-0	Tom Thomson	Jim Poling Sr.
1-55153-976-4	Trailblazing Sports Heroes	Joan Dixon
1-55153-977-2	Unsung Heroes of the RCAF	Cynthia J. Faryon
1-55153-987-X	Wilderness Tales	Peter Christensen
1-55153-990-X	West Coast Adventures	Adrienne Mason
1-55153-948-9	War of 1812 Against the States	Jennifer Crump
1-55153-873-3	Women Explorers	Helen Y. Rolfe

These titles are available wherever you buy books. If you have trouble finding the book you want, call the Altitude order desk at 1-800-957-6888, e-mail your request to: orderdesk@altitudepublishing.com or visit our Web site at www.amazingstories.ca

All titles retail for $9.95 Cdn or $7.95 US. (Prices subject to change.)

New AMAZING STORIES titles are published every month. If you would like more information, e-mail your name and mailing address to: amazingstories@altitudepublishing.com.